# *Pathfinding:*
## *Seven Principles for Positive Living*

# More Praise for Patricia Raskin and Pathfinding:
## Seven Principles for Positive Living

"Some books you may read once, put on the shelf, and rarely, if ever, look at them again. *Pathfinding: Seven Principles for Positive Living* is not one of those. Don't put it on the shelf. Keep it handy, where you can pick it up at any time and get a refresher course in positive living. Having written several books on self-esteem and positive living, I didn't think that Patricia Raskin could teach me anything new. I was wrong. This book contains gems of practical wisdom that can benefit everyone. A word of advice: Don't lend this book to anyone. You'll never get it back."

> Rabbi Abraham J. Twerski, M.D., Founder and Medical Director, Gateway Rehabilitation Center; and author of *Life's Too Short* and *Addictive Thinking*

"What I love most about Patricia Raskin's book, *Pathfinding: Seven Principles for Positive Living*, is its generosity of spirit. For over twenty years, Patricia has been a dedicated student and an impressive researcher in the field of positive living, and in this book, she gives her readers the benefit of her sizable and seasoned wisdom. Pathfinding is chock-full of memorable stories, rich in the pathos of the human condition. Patricia's warmth and articulate voice shine through as she teaches us both the inspiring and pragmatic principles for living more real, more engaging, and more passionate lives. This book gives us reason for hope in troubled times!"

> Gail Straub, Executive Director, Empowerment Training Programs and author of *Rhythm of Compassion* and *Empowerment: The Art of Creating Your Life As You Want It*

"Can there be too many books on finding our way in this complex world? Not while we continue to struggle with questions about our sense of place and purpose here. We often find our own paths through the deceptively simple stories of others who have gone before us in failure and success. *Pathfinding* is full of the kinds of stories that remind us not only of who we can *be,* but who we are."

Jon Wilson, Publisher & Editor-in-Chief, HOPE magazine

"After reading *Pathfinding: Seven Principles for Positive Living,* you'll want to celebrate the dance of life! Patricia Raskin has given us just what we need to find our path for positive living. Through moving thoughts from guests on her shows and her father's ancient wisdom, we learn how to apply these timeless truths. Her principles give us the workable formula for connecting, giving, forgiving, and miraculous living. Thank you, Patricia, for giving each of us the opportunity to experience the miracle of positive living."

Jackie Waldman, author of *The Courage To Give: Inspiring Stories of People Who Triumphed Over Tragedy to Make a Difference in the World*

"This book is filled with positive energy, wisdom and goodness. It offers an enthusiastic affirmation and celebration of life. Buy it for someone you love; but first, read it for yourself!"

Michael J. Gelb, author of *How to Think Like Leonardo daVinci* and *Discover your Genius*

"Every so often a book on personal development stands out as clearly exceptional with great ideas, great stories to illustrate those ideas and so well written that your soul urges you to keep turning the pages. *Pathfinding* and it's seven principles will delight you to the core of your being."

Louis A. Tartaglia, M.D., author of *The Great Wing* and *Flawless! Ten Character Flaws and What You Can Do About Them*

"Patricia Raskin's book, *Pathfinding: Seven Principles for Positive Living*, is both inspirational and practical. An awesome combination. I especially loved Chapter 7, 'Believe in Miracles.' I invite you to read and be inspired as I was."

Reverend Beth Curtis,
Crystal Coast Unity Church

"Patricia Raskin's inspirational masterpiece, *Pathfinding: Seven Priniciples for Positive Living*, has made her the Queen Bee of 'positive pollination.' In *Pathfinding*, she teaches all of us how to turn life's lemons into lemonade. Her book is an invaluable read to rejuvenate the spirit."

John Kelly, CSW, CAS, Executive Clinical Director, ExtraCare Health Services and author of *Warning Signs: A Guidebook for Parents*

# Pathfinding:
## Seven Principles for Positive Living

## Patricia J. Raskin, M.Ed.

Foreword by Melvin N. Raskin, DMD

Cover Artwork and Design: Rodney Shane Willis

Liberty Publishing Group
Egg Harbor • Frederick • Raleigh

Library of Congress Cataloging-in-Publication Data.

Raskin, Patricia J.
  Pathfinding : seven principles for positive living / Patricia J. Raskin. -- 1st ed.
  p. cm.
  ISBN 1-893095-13-4

  1. Self-actualization (Psychology)  2. Conduct of life.  3. Optimism.  4. Motivation (Psychology)
  I. Title

BF637.S4R37 2002                    158.1
    QBI33-559

           10  9  8  7  6  5  4  3  2  1

# Dedication

*To the two most important men in my life –*
*my father, Dr. Melvin Raskin and*
*my husband, Dr. Antonio Carbonell*

# Acknowledgements

There are so many people who have contributed to the transformation of my ideas to the reality of this book. My deepest gratitude and thanks go to:

My father, Dr. Melvin Raskin, for his incredible insights, wisdom and wonderful stories which add a rich and unique quality to this book.

My husband, Dr. Antonio Carbonell, for always understanding my purpose, believing in me and reminding me of my talents and gifts; and for his astute additions in the final editing stages of this book.

Cher and Bil Holton, my publishers, writing coaches, editors, dearest friends and consummate role models of how to live life to the fullest and give to others along the way.

armand huet de grenier, one of my first enlightened teachers, for introducing me to shamanic traditions where I discovered the honey bee as my power symbol.

Bobbi Gemma, my personal and professional coach and cherished friend, for always being there and supporting me.

Donita Todd, for embracing my philosophy and giving me my first opportunity to host my own program on a network television affiliate.

Walter and Lockwood Phillips, co-owners of the Carteret News-Times and WTKF-the Talk Station, for giving me the opportunity to host and produce my "Positive Living" radio program and to write the newspaper column, from which flowed many of the stories in the book.

Pam Phillips, for her steadfast support of my work and her idea to write a column based on the Positive Living show.

Germaine Biringer, for her faithful critique of my radio program each week, her friendship and her strong belief in my vision.

Dr. Lou Tartaglia for his knowledge, pearls of wisdom and stories when he co-hosted Positive Living and for encouraging me during the writing process.

Ann Barton, for being a faithful listener and contributor to Positive Living, where she brings her uplifting energy, beautiful poetry and authentic love of life.

My brother Russell Raskin, for reviewing the manuscript and giving me feedback which led me to make important clarifications in the biblical adaptations and spiritual concepts.

Amanda Dagnino, my copy editor, for her keen eye and detailed review of the manuscript.

Shane Willis, operations manager at WTKF and artist, for his technical expertise and support of my radio program from its inception, and for his ability to capture my conceptual idea into the beautiful book cover illustration.

The inspirational guests and contributors, for their knowledge and stories, without which this book would not have been written.

My own self-talk from a much higher source, for continually nudging me to complete this book, expand my work and to remain true to my calling of "pollinating" positive living through the airwaves.

# Table of Contents

# Foreword

*A*s parents, we are proud of our children's success. That's the easy part of parenting. The difficult part of parenting is being just as proud and loving of your children when things don't go right for them and they suffer the agonies and pains of life's adversities. I am especially proud of my daughter because she has been able to extract, organize and assemble the positive aspects of both the successes and failures of life. In this book, the reader is presented with those principles, ideas and beliefs by which she has lived.

The following story exemplifies those episodes in life which provide us with the opportunity to turn obstacles into opportunities. I hope it will help you capture the essence of my daughter's journey toward becoming the extraordinary person she is today.

> *One day the owner of a building tells his caretaker that he must go out of town for a day, but that he expects a most important letter. He informs the caretaker that he must make sure he gets the registered letter himself because it is a very important letter.*
>
> *The owner leaves the next morning. That afternoon the letter is delivered, but requires a signature. The caretaker tells the postman that he doesn't know how to write.*

> *The postman explains that he must obtain an actual signature, no marks or X's. Since the caretaker can't write, the postman refuses to leave the letter.*
>
> *When the owner returns and learns what happened, he becomes furious and fires the caretaker on the spot. The caretaker finds himself without a job and without an income. To support his meager existence, he starts peddling whatever goods and services he can to survive. His business begins to grow and improves to the point that he is able to open a little store.*
>
> *By the time his sons are old enough to help him, he has become well established. The sons inherit the business when the caretaker retires and decide to build a larger store. They ask their father to help them borrow the money to finance their ambitious undertaking.*
>
> *The father asks the banker for the loan and the banker says, "No problem. You can have whatever you need. Just sign on the dotted line."*
>
> *The caretaker looks at the banker and replies, "I can't sign. I never learned how to write."*
>
> *In astonishment, the banker asks, "How is it possible that a man who can't write could amass the wealth that you have?"*
>
> *"Ah," says the caretaker, "If I could write, I'd still be a caretaker."*

If Patricia had been able to "sign-on" to a perfect childhood, adolescence and adulthood, she would have become quite a different person. Trials, disappointments and tragedies are all part of life. Overcoming them builds character.

My daughter has become a woman of depth. As a pioneer in presenting positive living programs through radio, television, and print media, Patricia has touched the lives of thousands of people. The guests on her show are role models for positive, purposeful living. This book is an extension of what she has learned from her guests on those shows, her family, her heritage, and her own life experiences.

I hope you will take Patricia's perceptions and wisdom to heart. Use them to set your course in a more positive direction, and to reaffirm your own journey toward positive living.

It is truly fulfilling to have a child – your adult child – come to you with some of the things you taught her and realize they *took*. The foundation of a child's respect for parents and society is the greatest strength a culture can have.

I hope you will add my daughter's insights and wisdom to your own self-development curriculum. "Teach them diligently unto thy children, and to thy children's children."

Melvin N. Raskin, DMD

*Melvin Raskin, DMD, was one of the founders and the lay leader of the Jewish Center of Marco Island Florida. For fourteen years he led weekly and High Holy Day religious services, served as ritual chairman, and performed duties normally fulfilled by a rabbi.*

*After practicing dentistry for twenty-five years in Hartford, Connecticut, Dr. Raskin became a corporate officer of New York Blue Cross/Blue Shield overseeing the installation of dental insurance plans. He was one of the pioneers in the creation of dental insurance and traveled extensively lecturing on the subject.*

*Dr. Raskin is a veteran of World War II and a retired lieutenant colonel in the US Air Force Reserves. In his lifetime, he has served on the boards of his religious institutions and as president of his dental society and fraternity.*

*Currently Dr. Raskin is on the board of the Marco Health Care Center, an affiliate of Naples Community Hospital. He has been married for 58 years to Elaine Raskin and they have three children and nine grandchildren.*

# Introduction

*I*n *Pathfinding: Seven Principles for Positive Living* I present the fruits of a daughter's quest for selfhood and awakening. I include teachings, stories and lessons from important people and events in my life. I explore the importance of understanding the impact our heritage has on our own core beliefs and values. I share how our religious and cultural heritages affect our evolving personality and self-concept. I demonstrate how we can turn self-defeating attitudes and beliefs that we may have adopted during our youth into self-affirming statements of self-worth.

Over the past twenty years, I have focused on the positive side of living through the television and radio programs I have produced. As a result of my research and interviews with hundreds of people, I have come to some conclusions about positive living and positive people. I believe that we have five basic wants that go beyond food, clothing and shelter, and that balancing these wants is a life long process. The five basic wants are security – both financial and emotional; recognition – both personal and professional; safety; health, as in well-being; and peace-of-mind. I believe that external success is achieved through education, hard work and experience; internal success is achieved through self-acceptance. I feel that people who live positively have met life's challenges with both internal and external success.

I found my path to positive living from exploring the challenges and lessons associated with my childhood; my own life experience; my professional work evolution from being a teacher and guidance counselor to media producer and author; and from interviews with the extraordinary people who appear on my shows. My mother was the singer and dancer in me – the artistic *me*, the theatrical *me*, the show host *me*. My father was the disciplinarian and nurturer all in one. He brought out the seeker in me and taught me to always do the right thing and stand up for my beliefs.

*The Ethics of the Fathers* states, "Its not up to you to complete the job, but you must start it." My father adds, "Don't say I'll never be able to finish this. That doesn't hold. Start it. If you're building something, you are building it for the next generation." That's what I hope to do in this book.

*Pathfinding: Seven Principles for Positive Living* is a collection of the insights I've gained from my "beehive" ministry. My positive living and positive people shows are my beehives. Like the bee that draws nectar from deep inside the flower to make honey, I host positive living shows to draw the positive, life-enriching "nectar" from the life experiences of my guests. My shows become "beehives" of cross-pollination which transfer my guests' life experiences into food for thought, so my audiences can turn their own life experiences into a honey comb of strength, hope and positive action.

The bee analogy has become a personal symbol for my life's work. Through my media programs I am able to capture the "nectar" in people's lives and carry it over the airwaves to spread positive insights and principles that can change people's lives forever. The bee also symbolizes being able to do the impossible because anatomically it should not be able to fly. When I first began my "positive media" work as a pioneer, I was told that my approach would never sell because people wanted to hear the negative sensationalism. I have persistently and consistently stayed with my vision and production of positive living programs that are inspirational and solution based. I patiently waited and now we have come to a time and place where positive stories and inspiration are popular in publications, media, and movies.

We are living in a time where our level of trust is being strained – and even eroded – by the religious, political and financial institutions which have defaulted on their basic principles on which our country's foundation was built. I indeed feel honored to have been given the opportunity to produce and host media programs that allow me to be the beekeeper, "buzz through the air waves" to help spread sweetness, and to lift people toward positive living in a world which has been shaken by negativity.

The major sources of my "nectar" gathering for this book are the wisdom, insights and reflections I've gained from my father's stories, guests on my show, and my own life experiences. In Richard Bach's classic book *Illusions*, Jonathan Livingston Seagull says,"We teach others what we need to learn most for ourselves." This has become my motto, because what I have needed to learn most has led me to my life's work.

As I approach the next bend in my life-long journey, I want to leave a roadside marker for other seekers so they won't lose their way. This book is that roadside marker. I hope you will use it to take positive steps toward your own life's work.

My father wrote the Foreword to my book, which is a testimony to our shared admiration and respect. To have his enthusiastic support – as well as my mother's – means the world to me. Without my parents' presence in my life and without my husband Antonio's unbelievable support and guidance, as well as the incredible people I've interviewed over the years, this book would never have been written.

Many of the positive lessons my father taught me are in this book. His stories come from his childhood, his career and his work as a lay rabbi. The seven positive principles I outline are the result of my upbringing, outgoing and outreach. I have felt a sense of completeness and a higher sense of self emerge as a result of writing this book. I have found the words of Martha Borst, president of Phoenix 2000 and lecturer on self-discovery, to be true. She explains, "Until we are complete with our parents, we cannot be complete with ourselves."

My pathfinding has taught me a few things about family relationships. It has taught me appreciation, joy, patience, tolerance and acceptance. I have learned that my parents are human, that they did the best they could, that none of us are perfect – but we're perfect for each other. And we can be loved for who we are. That is the self-acceptance I personally found during the journey that produced this book.

The first chapter, "Honor Your Heritage," asks you to honor your cultural roots. Reaching back into your past holds the key to your future. It helps you appreciate how you evolved from your ethnicity, its traditions and customs. Chapter Two, "Be in the Precious Present," explores how each moment in our lives is a snapshot in time. Each precious moment becomes a blueprint for positive living, an affirmation for imprinting positive outlooks, and a platform for counting our blessings.

Chapter Three, "Use Your Imperfections to Perfect Your Life," addresses how we learn from our mistakes, work through anger and fear, regain our incredible personal power, use own inner strength to guide us, and rewrite our personal narratives through loving acts of kindness and forgiveness. Chapter Four, "Use Your Innate Gifts, Talents and Abilities," encourages us to honor our gifts and express the intrinsic qualities that make us unique human beings, be true to our purpose, set realistic stretch goals and be prepared to change and grow. Chapter Five, "Focus on the Positive," introduces the principle that you find good by surrounding yourself with positive people, positive places and positive things. I include real life examples and stories to show you how to find sources of inspiration, use visualization to help produce desired outcomes, and choose positive role models to bring peace, balance and harmony into your life.

In Chapter Six, "Respect and Protect Positive Relationships," the impact of relationships and how we use them to weave the fabric of our lives into a tapestry of togetherness is presented using delightful vignettes, illustrations and stories. This chapter shows how relationships must be nurtured, appreciated and protected – warts and all. The final chapter, "Believe in Miracles," tells us to let miracles point the way. It encourages us to find the miraculous in the ordinary. It includes stories about modern-day miracles and their lasting effects on people's lives.

It is my goal to offer readers inspiration, wisdom, suggestions, and solutions to issues they face in their daily lives. The issues presented in this book affect us all, and the underlying message is that we all have the ability to create positive experiences and achieve both internal and external success in our lives while working through life's challenges.

*Beehiving* this book has been a joy. Use the honey that you find to sweeten someone else's life. My father says, "We all have little tests, side roads, detours and bypasses. Everybody's trip is different, but we are all on the same road." My journey down that road has produced this book. I'm leaving it here, at the roadside for you. I haven't left it here for you to follow me. I've left it so  you can use it to follow your own heart, to take it back to your own hive, to sweeten your life and those dearest to you. And if you hear a buzz in your ear, it just might be your inner child whispering, "Enjoy your quest toward positive living."

# CHAPTER ONE

# ɧonor Ƴour ɧeritage

*We are born at a given moment; in a given place; and like vintage years of wines, we have the qualities of the year and of the season in which we are born.*               (C. G. Jung)

Our heritage holds the key to the historical us, but it also helps define the present us and even the future us. Recognizing and understanding our roots helps connect us with who we are and where we come from. Our lineage is the basis for our individuality, our uniqueness and our potential. The phrase "it's in the genes" is often used to describe the character traits we have in common with other members of our family.

Our genes are part of our biological narrative. And while they don't tell our whole story, they are an important part of it. That's why I believe we should honor our heritage. We should think about it, listen to stories about it, tell stories about it, and write about it.

Understanding our ancestral connections, our family's genealogical roots and our predecessor's stories constitutes the foundation of our very being. How can we truly appreciate where we're going unless we know – and appreciate – where we've been? Honoring our heritage is honoring our past, and honoring our past is honoring our future.

*Find Your Legacy*

*Our legacy is an omnibus in which all our
ancestors ride.* (Oliver Wendell Holmes)

*I* have been reminded by my father that it's important
to apply ancient teachings to modern every day
society and ask ourselves where they fit, what they teach us
and how they can help us. In living a good life, the common
threads are persisting, listening, learning and putting yourself in the right position. All these are positives no matter
who you are or where you come from. I have adopted that
philosophy and continue to value the lessons my heritage
has taught me. My father's admonition to ask ourselves
where ancient teachings fit into our current world view carries considerable intellectual weight. We must learn old
lessons before we can reap new benefits. Learning from the
past is earning from the past. The dividends of the positive
lessons we've learned are the currency of our future.

Stephen Pavuk, a guest on my radio program and co-
author of *The Story of a Lifetime: A Keepsake of Personal
Memoirs* sums up the overall benefits of preserving family
histories through writing. "The benefit of all this overflows
from the one who writes the memoirs. People learn from
that person. They begin to see the good qualities in that person. It's sort of like the ripple on the pond when you throw
a rock in," he said. "It just flows into their families. It flows
beyond that out into the world and then it flows to their
descendants, to future generations. The benefits are both
immediate and long-lasting." This rock that causes the ripples is the weight of our own special heritage as we throw
ourselves into the pool of life. We cause ripples by jumping,

character first, into a world of characters who have their own heritage to honor or neglect.

As I uncovered stories of my heritage through my father, I caught a glimpse into my past and an understanding of why I was taught certain lessons. I learned why I have made the choices that I have and why I focus on positive outcomes instead of negative consequences. For example, here is a story he tells:

> *Whenever we stayed with my grandmother, she would always tell us a story about a little boy and girl who, while walking through the woods, found a little boy who was crying. When they asked him why he was crying, he said he was hungry, so they took him home, made sure he ate and then they brought him to his own home. My grandmother's story was intended to emphasize that the Torah (the Hebrew Bible) teaches us to perform mitzvahs (Hebrew word for kind deed or considerate act.)*
>
> *Now this is probably true in all religions, but in Judaism the purpose of mankind is to do good in the world. The phrase in Hebrew is Tikkun Olam, which means to repair the world. The Kabbalah, which is a book of ancient Hebrew mysticism, likens the whole picture of life to a king who creates a beautiful castle with magnificent rooms, exquisite furniture, gourmet foods and fully-stocked libraries, yet no one comes to enjoy them. He waits his entire life for people to taste of the fruits of his labors. This is true of life, where we do not make use of all the good things that are available to us.*

I believe the ultimate purpose of my radio show, my bee ministry, is Tikkun Olam (to repair the world). My seven principles for positive living are the chief tools in the repair kit. The guests on my show help mend people's lives. We invite listeners to my "media garden" to enjoy the *nectar* of the positive messages my show promotes.

In the following story told by my father, I learned that the traits I inherited explain my drive for doing what I feel is right in my heart:

*In Czarist Russia, most Jews were orthodox, and Jewish boys attended their own schools, called Yeshivas. There was a military draft for all boys of military age. When Jewish boys were drafted into the Czars' army, they were treated as inferiors. They could not obtain Kosher foods. So it wasn't surprising that many of the Jewish boys facing military service left Russia before they could be drafted. Where did they go? They went to America.*

*Your grandfather, as a youth, traveled all over Siberia. He was an entrepreneur and a salesman, so it wasn't surprising that when he faced the draft he decided to leave Russia and go to America. He sewed five hundred dollars into the lining of his coat. That is all that he owned. He kissed his mother goodbye, said goodbye to his friends, and left for America.*

*At that time there was an underground that operated throughout Europe, and it was able to spirit Jewish boys from town to town westward until they got to the German border. Once they got to Germany, they could board a ship that was*

> *bound for America. Your grandfather got all the way across Poland, and at the last Jewish outpost of the underground there was a family who had an eligible daughter. Her father took a fancy to your grandfather and demanded that he marry his daughter. But your grandfather didn't want to marry his daughter. They threatened him that if he didn't marry her, they would turn him in to the authorities. So during that night, he sneaked out and escaped.*
>
> *He made his own way across Germany, got on a ship from Germany and came to New York. Later when he settled in America, he brought some of his family over, including your great-grandmother. Your great-grandfather died in Russia.*
>
> *Your grandfather left New York and came to Boston with the help of people he knew from the old country. There he started his own business and proceeded to raise his own family.*

My grandfather left an incredible legacy and his courage and persistence are qualities that define each generation of our family. I'd like to think some of his courage, and my parents' persistence, have rubbed off on me. Perhaps my positive living philosophy is my way of helping people move from an underground existence to a steppingstone life. I hope so. If my seven principles for positive living can be steppingstones for people who seek personal freedom and selfhood, then I can't think of a better way to honor my grandfather's incredible voyage to America.

One of my most memorable moments as a child, was listening to my grandmother tell Russian folk tales as we sat nestled on the bed. I vividly remember her story about a poor, hungry woman who knocked on the door of a stranger to ask for a piece of bread and some water. When she was turned away, the person who refused to offer her food was plagued with frogs or snakes which jumped out of his mouth whenever he tried to speak. However, if the poor woman was welcomed by the host when she knocked on his door, gold and pearls would come out of the host's mouth whenever he spoke.

My grandmother's message was clear: Perform kind deeds whenever you can. Be loving and kindhearted. Treat people kindly so you will be treated kindly. Speak pearls of wisdom. Respect people. Be compassionate because the pattern of the human race goes from individual to family to group to community to city to state to nation to the world. What is passed from one is passed to all. What is done to one affects everyone. I cherish the times I spent at her side soaking up the stories and heritage she passed on to me.

My family heritage is my personal, cultural and professional foundation. It's my moral, ethical and spiritual compass. In novels, movies and plays, historical and chronological time frames are the keys to character development. Just as historical foundations set the stage in the arts, our heritage serves as the foundation for our lives. We cannot fully understand our lives without comprehending the context of our beginnings.

As we seek to understand and appreciate those who came before us, we step out of our own personal narratives and into theirs. We step back in time intellectually and emotionally to get a sense for what influenced them in their youth and adulthood. We wonder how our ancestors handled their challenges and struggles. Most of all, we begin to understand them as people, as human beings trying to find their way in a world that was different, yet strikingly similar to the world we inhabit.

I am convinced that more families would stay together if they would honor stories about the exploits and achievements of family members. These treasure troves of family history should be preserved and handed down as legacies to all succeeding generations. To unlock these generational narratives is to set our family history free. It is an invitation to honor those who came before us.

In one of my discussions about our family's heritage, my father related:

> *My parents came from the Old World setting, from the ghettos in Europe where religion was the mainstay of existence. When they got to this country, they found that they were free to worship in their own way without religious restrictions. Your great-grandmother had two sisters and four brothers and the family was very close. We always had a place to go to visit. Even to this day, my last remaining first cousin with whom I am close, still calls me. This seemingly insignificant occurrence is a constant reminder of our family roots. It reminds me of where I came from and what our family values are. Loyalty and closeness to each other so that the links of family will be maintained even after we parents pass on. And that link connects the children to values of their ancestors, which is a constant reminder of family standards for them to live up to. Once the parents are gone, that immediate source is gone and the only source left is family links.*

This was really impressed upon us as children, and today my brothers and I are very close. Even though we are a thousand miles apart, we stay in contact regularly.

When I pressed my father further to compare the teachings of his parents to those he passed on to us, he explained, "I gave you what I got." He then told me a specific lesson my grandmother taught him.

*I vaguely remember an incident where I was bragging about something I had done in front of several children and their parents. But I vividly remember your grandmother taking me aside and lovingly scolding me with the admonition that one is never to show off, brag, or behave in such a way as to evoke jealously in other people.*

*She impressed upon me the importance of being considerate of other people, to understand where the other person is coming from before your criticize or get angry about anything that they have done to you.*

*I see this in you, in how you react to us as your parents. You have always been considerate of us and show us you care even when you are too busy or far away to be with us.*

To hear my father compliment me like that in the context of our discussion about our family history was a special and very meaningful moment. It made me feel that this behavior was really an inherent trait and part of what has been passed down to me through the generations.

It's interesting how many similarities there are between family generations. I reminded my father about his granddaughter's birthday when my daughter Laura was just a small child. She was being showered with unusually large numbers of gifts, which she delighted in opening. I asked my father if he remembered the incident. "Yes," he said, "I told you that Laura shouldn't open all of those gifts in front of the other children because it might make some of them jealous." Then he recounted a story from his boyhood:

*At age thirteen, Jewish tradition holds that a boy attains manhood by reading from the Holy Torah, the Hebrew Bible, which is not an easy task and requires special training. At my Bar Mitzvah I did very well.*

*My parents held a modest celebration in which all of the relatives were crammed into our little apartment on the third floor of a three-story building. Everybody was happy and they were praising me about what a great job I had done. They all wanted to hear from me, the Bar Mitzvah boy.*

*After I made my speech, people praised me for the great job I had done and commented on how I was going to go on to bigger and better things. However, in the middle of all of these praiseworthy remarks my uncle, who had not done well compared to other members of the family, very somberly remarked, 'Wait a minute. Why are we praising this boy? We don't know how he is going to turn out.'*

*I'll never forget that, for in that joyous moment, he exhibited a sour grapes attitude, which I interpreted as his saying, 'You may be praising him today, but will you be praising him tomorrow?' In other words, 'Don't brag about what he's doing now. Let's see how he turns out before we praise him.'*

That story struck very close to home for me. "Dad, you do that with us," I said. "You don't look at the individual incident. You always hold judgment. You withhold praise."

He responded, "That's absolutely right. My uncle's words stuck with me all these years. That is the reason I say to my children, 'Don't brag about it. Wait for results. I don't want you to be disappointed if things don't work out as you expect.'"

I said, "I don't agree. I often felt that you did not appreciate my accomplishments."

"I would rather praise the result and not worry about the interim effort because I expect that you can't get the result without the effort," he countered good-naturedly.

"But in the effort, there are successes along the way," I replied.

"That may be, but the end result is what you are working for. You're not working for interim success. I have tasted the bitterness of disappointment. It is stronger than the joy of elation. So you must focus on results and not the interim steps. But you cannot lose sight of the fact that even when you get the recognition for the ultimate result, there is always more to be accomplished. I was the result of my Bar Mitzvah, but that result, the new me, was just a process to my uncle."

"I can see your point, Dad, but to me, the process is as important as the result, because success comes from the process of events preceding the final result."

I have come to realize I had interpreted a proud father's pragmatic detachment and limited praise for my accomplishments as disinterest and apathy. But his reticence to shower me with compliments was his way of preventing me from resting on my laurels. I discovered that each of my accomplishments has been a monument to my worth, a testimony to a father's faith in his daughter, a steppingstone toward my life's work.

Although my father has been economical with his praise through the years, I understand his intentions. He wants to fortify me, to toughen me up; to produce a daughter who values the work to be done more than the work accomplished. He has influenced me as I have influenced my daughter, Laura. She has told me that I go after my dreams and have taught her to believe in herself and to go for her own dreams. And I watch her pursue her higher education as well as her work as an activist to increase racial tolerance and promote a more cooperative society. She strives to make the world a better place to live. Her work is an extension of mine and her "pathfinding" encompasses a global scope.

I think that the importance of knowing our family heritage is that we seek out how the generations before us did it, which helps us to do it better.

I encourage you – whoever you are, whatever family background you come from, wherever you are going – to honor the heritage and legacy that is yours and yours alone. Share family stories. Allow your common family history to draw you closer together. Don't miss any opportunity to visit and vacation with relatives. Let the remembrances you share be monuments to your family's storied heritage.

Explore remote, almost forgotten family paths together. Pathfinding is a family-enrichment activity. It has the same effects as family prayer – it holds families together. It establishes the links for passing family torches from generation to generation.

Each generation has to learn important lessons from the previous one. That willingness to learn from each other and apply the family lessons will produce the dividends of sound family values and philosophies. In this way, each generation leaves its own legacy.

# Accept and Appreciate Your Past

*Look not mournfully into the past. It comes not back again. Wisely improve the present. It is thine. Go forth to meet the shadowy future, without fear and with a brave heart.*

(Henry Wadsworth Longfellow)

Our family histories are warehouses of beliefs, values, achievements, secrets, philosophies, successes and failures. These multidimensional qualities are at the core of a family's past, present and future. Those of us who are current products of our family's lineage stand at the apex of all of the accumulated family experience. We are the heirs of our heritage, of everything our families have accomplished to date. Families who have a strong sense of heritage know it is safe to look within, to examine family values as well as family secrets and to make peace with the family history.

I feel fortunate enough to say that every time I look deeper into my own family history, I find special family treasures. In writing this book and tapping into my father's wisdom, I realized that the musical and artistic talents bestowed upon my brothers and me have been handed down by several generations of my family on both sides. My great-uncle, my grandfather Louis' brother, was part of a husband and wife Russian dance team. My father's cousin, Arnold Archer, has been in show business for sixty years. My maternal grandmother was a talented seamstress who designed and made my mother's and aunt's clothes from scratch without patterns.

My mother's cousin is a talented artist and my mother and her twin sister, Aunt Myrtle, have been musicians since childhood. They have sung, played the piano and performed in their respective communities.

All of this has helped me appreciate what was passed down to me. Growing up, our home was constantly filled with music. There were two baby grand pianos in the living room, which were played by my brother Paul and my mother. I was a child singer and was always being accompanied by my mother or singing duets with her. To me this was the norm because I didn't know any other way. But as I grew up I realized that the music in our family was our self-expression and our joy, and was unique to us. I believe that this artistic gift has been handed down to us. My brother Paul is a very talented designer, musician, actor and producer. My work is in the media, and although I'm not singing any more, I use my speaking voice on my radio program.

One of the strengths of my family is that we care about one another. We keep in constant touch. We listen to each other. We have a strong work ethic. Shying away from a challenge or difficult circumstances isn't part of our family's vocabulary. We trust in an abiding faith. We believe all things work together for good, and that a Divine Hand supports us and guides us.

My brother, Russell, has carried on the religious traditions of our heritage. He and his wife, Deborah, have eight children and are Orthodox Jews. Although all three of us siblings have very different lifestyles, we all love and accept each other. Because every one of our family members is unique, we meet each other on the common ground of our own heritage. We believe part of our birthright is to express who we are and to honor and value our individual differences, and we have a great respect for each other.

All families have their ups and downs, successes and failures, shining moments and dull moments. There are always a few things we wish we could have done differently. But in exploring your family heritage, you can find things that you managed to do extraordinarily well that are unique to your family.

## *Capture Your Memories*

*Life can only be understood backward,*
*but it must be lived forward.* (Niels Bohr)

*S*tep back into memory lane once in a while. Experience snapshots of your past that help you appreciate your heritage. Bask as often as you can in fond memories of important events in your family's history. Cher Holton, Ph.D., author of *Living at the Speed of Life: Staying in Control in a World Gone Bonkers,* says, "Remembered joys enrich the present. They take our minds off our present labors and ground us to that part of us that knows what joy feels like. Pleasant memories fortify us from today's labors. They center us. They remind us we are capable of feeling joy and experiencing inner peace."

Dr. Holton captures the essence of the therapeutic effect that fond memories have on present circumstances. All of us have the ability to mentally step out of our present dilemmas and worries. We can concentrate on pleasant memories from our past by looking through family photo albums, watching videos of family get-togethers, visiting or calling grandparents, re-reading old letters and other vintage correspondence, colorizing old family snapshots and duplicating them for the family, researching family trees, and more.

There are many things we can do to create and capture cherished memories including holding family reunions,

20

organizing multi-generational vacations, taking group pictures, publishing family albums, creating multi-generational family cookbooks, recording family stories and superstitions.

Some families write family histories, poetry or songbooks to capture words, thoughts and achievements of family members. Heirlooms are passed from generation to generation. Some families chronicle family achievements similar to those catalogued in the *Guinness Book of Records*. A few families place notes, cards, letters and mementos in specially-designed "time-capsules" for future generations. Voices are recorded for posterity. Quilts are made from clothing and bequeathed to following generations. Portraits are painted and inherited.

On Positive Living, I interviewed Stephen Pavuk, co-author of *The Story of a Lifetime: A Keepsake of Personal Memoirs*. His book is a personal biographical framework of questions, which elicit the stories, memories and philosophies of loved ones in their own words. His unique gift book was awarded the Seal of Quality by the Family Channel and named a "Top 15 Mother's Day Bestseller" by Ingram.

Mr. Pavuk talked about the power of the responses entered by beloved family members in the book. He said, "The experience they create can be life-changing and it starts because they begin to talk about what is important to them on the inside. They have more dialogue with family members about things they haven't talked about in many years, or perhaps ever. In terms of positive living, what they are really beginning to do is to speak their own truth and accept each other for doing that. In terms of understanding your heritage, there is great value in getting that kind of communication from your own family."

He also mentioned some of the questions in *The Story of a Lifetime* that evoke deep responses, such as, "Have you made peace with everyone important in your life? If you could change how you raised your children, what would you do differently? Is there something that you always wanted to do but never did? What do you feel has been your purpose in life?" He added, "What people begin to realize is that even though they think they know their parents, their grandparents, or their great-grandparents, they really don't know them as well as they assume. They remember their grandparents as these really nice people who bought them ice cream and took them places when they were kids. They have wonderful, nostalgic memories and warm feelings toward those special relatives who gave them a lot of attention, care and love, but they have little idea of what made them tick on the inside."

I asked what changes Mr. Pavuk sees in his own life since he has written this book. He said, "I'm communicating differently. When I look at the history of our family, I look at my relationship with my ancestors. For example, I think about important questions about my parents. I ask myself, 'What were they thinking as they faced certain challenges in their lives? What did they feel when they had a certain victory or triumph, got a promotion at work or a new house? What was their idea about raising children? What did my parents want for all of us as we came along into the world? What were their hopes and dreams and plans for the future?

"When you think about your parents that way, you think about yourself that way, too. You also think about other relationships, not only with your parents and grandparents, but with your spouse, your children and with others around you. All of this makes me more mindful in every moment of the choices I make, the things I say, and the actions I take day in and day out with everyone in my life. When you think that everything you do has an effect on everyone with whom you come in contact, you begin to realize the importance of living a better life, because those effects are far-reaching and long-lasting."

Mr. Pavuk concluded by saying that people have told him that as their loved ones are telling their stories in *The Story of a Lifetime*, they will remember things that happened early in their lives that meant so much to them. He said, "It may have been one little occurrence that happened with their children or their spouse that was a special moment in their life which is still with them today, many years later. This one little thing that happened to them had such a profound effect on them. Recording and sharing these moments help you see great value in your own life and in the lives of others."

During the writing of this chapter, I heard from a cousin with whom I had not spoken in twenty years. She found me on the Internet and was thrilled to connect again. I put her in touch with my parents and my father has answered her e-mail questions about her grandparents and relatives on our side of the family. She thanked him for telling her about her grandmother and how much she looked like her. It meant a lot to her to reestablish contact with our family.

This amazing Internet connection brought positive childhood memories to the forefront. It was especially meaningful because she contacted me while my parents were visiting, which they do once or twice a year. I believe that rekindling these connections and reliving those special moments make us more complete, contribute to our quality of life and add years to our lives.

Rick Nurrie Sterns and his wife, Mary, editors of *Soulful Living: The Process of Personal Transformation*, and guests on my radio program, discussed the importance of writing about our own personal history and building a portfolio of memories. "I think one of the most profound things people can do," he says, "is to sit down and write about their own personal history. It puts things in perspective and as a result, at least for myself, I gain freedom. I understand that I'm not going to stay where I am right now.

When we release through writing, what we hold on to emotionally, we gain perspective and we discover what new life awaits us."

For me, building a portfolio of family memories is a "life giving" project. Capturing important snapshots of our families through time acknowledges the foundation of our own growth and identity. Ralph Waldo Emerson puts it this way, "Each one of us finds room in a few square inches of our face for the traits of all our ancestors; for the expression of all our history, and our wants." Our attitudes, beliefs, values and physical characteristics are updates of our family album. We resemble our past as much as we want to reassemble our future. And we can only do that as Niels Bohr has said, "by understanding our life backwards."

I try to relive family memories through planning special events. For example, for the past two years I created a Passover Seder within our community. The attendance grew from 50 people the first year to 100 people the second year. The Seder is a festive evening which commemorates the Israelite's freedom from bondage. Family members gather, socialize and read the story in a book called the Haggadah. This is a special memory from my childhood, and I found it very gratifying to share the experience with those in the community who attended.

My parents traveled fifteen hours to be here so my father could lead the Seder. Last year, I wrote a newspaper article about this ecumenical event in our community. This year a reporter attended the Seder and my parent's picture appeared on the front page of our paper with the caption "Over 100 people attend Seder." In addition to strengthening my family roots and creating priceless memories, I was building a sense of community. Those moments will always be with me long after my parents are gone. I want to do all I can to capture special moments with my parents while they are here.

## *Respect Other People's Heritage*

*When we seek for connection, we restore the
world to wholeness. Our separate lives become
meaningful as we discover how truly necessary
we are to each other.*     (Margaret Wheatley)

*T*hrough my workshops and associations, I came
upon three stories that show the strength of family
and the timeless impact heritage can have. These incredible
stories exemplify the joy of honoring your heritage. The
first is of Julia Brown who shared her story with the group
in a seminar I was presenting. Julia Brown's story:

*It was November and I was in my 20's. I was young
and in love with a man who was to become my husband. He was doing his surgical residency in
Rochester, Minnesota. We were tired of a long distance relationship, so I quit my job as a nurse, packed
up all the belongings I could fit into my small car, and
drove to Minnesota.*

*The day before I left I visited my grandmother to
say goodbye. She was a South Dakotan, and was
accustomed to long hard winters. She offered to
accompany me, sensing I might need help with the
long drive. She turned out to be right. Within four
hours of leaving Vancouver, as we headed toward the*

*Rocky Mountains, we were enveloped in a severe winter storm that paralyzed the northwestern states. What was supposed to be a three-day car trip took seven days.*

*As we crept across Montana, Wyoming and South Dakota on our way to Minnesota, it turned out to be a beautiful opportunity to get to know my grandma as a person. I asked her questions about my father and grandfather. I was just astounded to see what a strong person my grandma was, and how she met all the adversities in her life head on and just carried on and conquered them. We became very, very close on that trip. My grandma gave me a wonderful gift of her time. I don't know what I would have done without her in the storm. Grandma always said that family is the most important thing. We often reminisced about our trip, and I told her how important she was to me. She was a pretty remarkable lady. She died at the age of 87.*

The second story is of Fran Travisano who I met at a workshop. I was struck by the fact that she and her whole family, including grandparents, parents and most of the children and grandchildren all lived within a three-mile radius of each other. They have stayed together, carrying on their family legacy. I wanted to know more about their physical and emotional closeness, and I asked her to explain it.

*My husband and I grew up as second generations Italians in a large family. Until my early teens I lived in a multi-family house in Jersey City owned by my grandparents who spoke very little English. One of the apartments was occupied by the daughter (and her family) of my grandmother's brother who lived next door in a multi-family house. On the same street lived another older cousin of theirs. Other uncles, aunts and cousins also lived in the city. Every Sunday we would visit the homes of aunts and uncles in other parts of New Jersey and New York and I got to know all of my 29 first cousins.*

*Friends and in-laws were also part of the extended family. Probably 95 percent of all those people were Italian, mostly first generation. There were no professionals among the aunts and uncles, just hardworking middle class people who deeply valued family life, loved God, and served their country during World War II. The native tongue was spoken by the older folks. Traditional foods were prepared, especially for the holidays. Weddings and other occasions were a chance to revive the folk dances.*

*Everyone's talents and accomplishments were encouraged, supported and praised. There was a certain comfort level in living in close proximity, as well as a sense of responsibility to our elders. So we followed the traditions of our upbringing with our children. There were lots of Sunday dinners and weddings. Every other week seemed to be a "special" occasion of birthdays, anniversaries, graduations and school or sports events.*

*We always endeavored to be open and honest with our children. We never withheld love and freely expressed annoyances, likes and dislikes. Volatility, loud voices and shouting were not uncommon. But love was always demonstrated both physically and verbally.*

*Our word is our bond. We say what we mean and mean what we say. Our children could always depend on our word. We are very quick to apologize and to take full responsibility for our actions. We are not reluctant to say no, and yet at the same time, will admit when we are wrong without fear of "losing face."*

*Adults are very active in their children's lives with homework, sports, church, etc. The men are involved in every aspect of household duties and child rearing. The prevalent values in my grandchildren's homes are love, honesty, respect of others (and their elders) and "pitching in." My grandchildren are raised very much the way we were raised – with lots of family and friends around. An important element that has kept the generations close is our mutual respect for each other. We have great fun being together. There are no major arguments that are not resolved quickly. We do not approve of everything, but we allow space for individuality.*

*Our grandparents, and indeed probably their grandparents, were raised in small villages in Italy where hard work and reliance on family and friends was the common environment. They naturally brought their way of living to America, settling near each other and counting on the family and/or friends who had arrived before them to ease the tremendous adjustments they faced. They lived near each other, worked near each other and played near each other. They loved each other. This was their legacy.*

The third story is Mary Madsen's story. She is a hair-dresser who was born and raised in Scotland. She told me about her family of twelve in her lovely and lilting Scottish brogue while I sat in her chair having my hair styled. This is her story:

*Being the oldest of twelve, I had more chores to do and more responsibilities. I helped my mother cook and sew. We knitted socks and gloves and made our dresses. My mother ran our home like a boarding house. Everyone shared everything. We sectioned our oranges, divided cake and cookies, poured half glasses of milk. I feel that people are too materialistic today. We never had much, so we shared everything we had. We never felt deprived though. We always felt rich.*

*Mother told us stories and sang to us. She was always there when any of us needed her. We struggled to make ends meet sometimes, but we never struggled to love each other. When we couldn't afford things, we didn't buy them. My parents taught all of us to be thrifty, healthy and hard-working. We loved to spend time together over a cup of coffee. I think people who lose touch with family lose touch with themselves.*

These snapshots of other people's heritage help me gain a whole new appreciation of the richness of cultural diversity and cultural similarities. We are more alike than different. Families want to provide emotional, physical, psychological, spiritual, financial and ethical anchors for their children.

Kahlil Gibran speaks about children in *The Prophet*, saying, "They come through you but not from you; and though they are with you, they belong not to you. You are the living bows from which your children as living arrows are sent forth."

The family is "the nucleus of civilization," says Will Durant. Without families, there wouldn't be such a thing as civilization. Family heritages fortify society with the strength of diversity. Honoring our heritage helps us to honor someone else's heritage. We can learn a lot from each other, grow with each other and do things for each other. Even if your extended family does not have an easily discernible history, you can begin with your own family now. Your children and grandchildren will bless you for it.

I will use the eloquence of Henry George to summarize this chapter. His wisdom honors all of our heritages and assures us that our attempts at pathfinding need the countless attempts at pathfinding by others. "Generations, succeeding to the gain of their predecessors," says George, "gradually elevate the status of (humankind), as coral polyps, building one generation upon the work of the other, gradually elevate themselves from the bottom of the sea."

## *Positive Pollination*

*List:*

- ❖ Positive traits that you've inherited from your parents/guardians.
- ❖ Positive traits that you see in family members and relatives.
- ❖ Positive traits that you want to pass on to your children.
- ❖ Phrases you learned from your family that you value and use.

*Reflect on:*

- ❖ The ways your family has done something to "repair the world," to make it a better place.
- ❖ Your family's traditions and customs that have influenced you the most.
- ❖ The chief values your parents taught you.
- ❖ The most joyful memories you have of your grandparents.
- ❖ Major turning points in your life.

# CHAPTER TWO

# Be In the Precious Present

*Live neither in the past nor in the future, but let*
*each day's work absorb your entire energies,*
*and satisfy your wildest ambitions.*

(William Osler)

*B*eing in the precious present, and trusting it, is the second principle for positive living. "If you pay attention at every moment," says Michael Ray, School of Business Manager, Stanford University, "you form a new relationship to time. In some magical way, by slowing down, you become more efficient, productive and energetic; focusing without distraction directly on the task in front of you. Not only do you become immersed in the moment, you become that moment."

This is an important life principle. If we could slow down enough to catch ourselves, we would sense our eternal connection with the present. We would realize the present moment is the only moment we have. To lose a sense for the present is to lose a sense for the future. Living fully in the present means changing your sight into insight. And as your insight deepens, you will sense the value of

33

each moment. You can discover the value of the precious present right now.

Brian Luke Seaward, a guest on my radio program, is the author of *The Art of Calm: Relaxation Through the Five Senses.* He uses relaxing sights, sounds, smells, tastes and touches to show us how to enjoy life's subtle treasures and discover delight in everyday routines. Dr. Seaward said, "The bottom line is to live in the present moment. We tend to live in the past with guilt and the future with worry. Although it is important to plan for the future, I think that we miss the present moment."

I really got to experience the 'precious present' on an Alaskan cruise my husband and I took.

*The majesty of the glaciers, the beauty of their turquoise blue color, the sound of the dolphins jumping in the water, the joy I felt from watching the otters bask in the sun on their own private "island," the smell of the ocean, and the amazing taste of the native salmon, were sensory experiences I will never forget and that stay with me today. My husband and I would sit for hours on the deck of the ship, mesmerized by the awesome beauty of the nature around us.*

*The cruise came at a time of great stress in our business, and I felt the romantic, emotional part of our relationship was waning. I knew the connection and "kindling fire" were there but burning on low, so we went on this cruise as a way of "adding a log to the fire" and recapturing our majesty and beauty together, and it worked. The Alaskan cruise provided an environment where we could totally immerse ourselves in the present, with each other.*

I also did some very powerful visualization exercises on the cruise to heal a sore throat I developed. I read the book of one of my guest authors, Mary Rockwood Lane, R.N., Ph.D. co-author of *Spirit Body Healing: Using Your Minds Eye To Unlock The Medicine Within*, the first book on spiritual healing to come from a research study in a major university health-care center. I followed an exercise in the book which helped me understand the discomfort in my body and work through it. *Spirit Body Healing* is based on a method of healing yourself taken from a research study at Shands Hospital from 1992 to 1999 at the University of Florida. A guest on my radio program, Dr. Lane talked about how individuals were able to work through pain by doing the exercises. "They would face and embody the pain. I feel that the place where there's a darkness in our lives is a three dimensional place. When you walk into that place it's like a space that is within you and there's a part of you that actually lives in there. I use guided imagery techniques in the book that allow you to go deeper into that place and at the same time experience it in a very safe and protected way. Using your breath and imagery techniques, you are able to work in that place and move from there."

Dr. Lane is talking about using visualization to find the source of your pain so that you can understand where it comes from. When I did the exercise, the pain intensified at first because I concentrated on it. Then, as I could "see" an image, which for me was sharp thin blades in my throat, my sore throat diminished and eventually disappeared.

On how people have healed themselves from illness using these techniques, Dr. Lane said, "There is a spirit mind body shift that actually happens in every cell of your body and also resonates with your whole spirit."

On the show, Dr. Lane gave listeners and readers a practical positive exercise to do. She said, "Allow yourself a few moments of your day and go into your inner space. Relax, let your breathing slow down, take several deep breaths, and as you breathe in and you breathe out, allow the feelings of relaxation, lightness and your edges to soften. In your imagination, take yourself to a place that you love. It could be a forest path, a beach, a favorite park. Feel yourself there. Feel the air on your face, the ground below your feet, and be there. Look around. Allow the feeling of peace to surround you. In this place listen. Listen to your own inner voice. It is your voice of wisdom. It is your voice of truth. Allow yourself to be with yourself. Feel yourself embraced within your own life. Take a few moments and allow the energy within you to expand and transform into lightness."

Dr. Caroline Myss, author of *Anatomy of the Spirit,* talks about how the seven different energy centers in our body hold energy. When you have pain in one of those centers, such as the head, back, knee or stomach, the energy in the center is being drawn away from that part of your body. For example, if your shoulder hurts, the theory is that the pain goes into the shoulder and you lose energy in your shoulder. When you feel disempowered, hurt, angry or are in pain, Dr. Myss instructs, in her tapes and books, how to use the signal from your body to help regain your power by "calling your power back."

In these few moments of self awareness, you are at the epicenter of the stream of life that courses through your body. "The same stream of life," says Rabindranath Tagore, "that runs through the world runs through (your) veins night and day and dances in rhythmic measure. It is the same life that shoots in joy through the dust of the earth into the numberless blades of grass and breaks into tumultuous waves of flowers." This kind of vibrancy is all around us, but most of the time, we miss it because we don't allow ourselves to enjoy the thousands of precious moments that come our way each day.

## *Use the Precious Present to Listen to and Practice Using Your Intuition*

*Be brave enough to live creatively. The creative place is where no one else has ever been. You have to leave the city of your comfort and go into the wilderness of intuition. You can't get there by bus, only hard work, risking, and by not quite knowing what you're doing.* (Alan Alda)

*S*taying "present in the moment" also means listening to your intuition. Ellen Fritz Solart, author of *Living Inside Out*, gave my listeners steps to develop the intuitive mind by strengthening the connection to the subconscious. Ms. Solart explained how intuition works. She said, "We all have the five senses, which are seeing, hearing, smelling, tasting and feeling. Anything which comes from those senses comes from what I call the outer authority. It comes from the world to us. The inner senses, which are inner hearing, inner sight, inner taste, and inner smell and feelings are what I call the inner voices or intuition." She gave an example: "On one of my trips, my head and outer authority told me to turn left, according to the map. But, I got a strong feeling that I should turn right, and I made that turn. I found out later that there was a bridge out and a detour that would have taken me way out of my way."

In *Success, Your Dream and You*, I wrote, "The voice inside us tells us when we are not listening. Our behavior gives us the answers. When we don't listen to our intuition, we lose time, energy and efficiency."

Florence Scovel Shinn writes, "Intuition is a spiritual faculty, and does not explain, but simply points the way." However, there are those who feel that intuition has more value when it is part of an educated guess. On Positive Living, Lynda Dahl, co-author of *The Book of Fallacies: A Little Primer of New Thought*, talked about the fallacy people believe about using your intuition: If I follow my impulses, they lead me astray. She said, "Somehow impulses have gotten a bad rap over the years. Impulses come from a deeper part of us which might be called our inner self. Impulses lead us in directions that are best suited to our own needs and desires. To deny impulses, or not follow them, closes doors that this greater part of us is trying to lead us to. For example, if we're looking for a new job and not following our impulses, we may not send our resume to a certain company when the impulse arises, logically justifying our action somehow. However, the impulse is coming from our inner self for a reason…and maybe that reason is an opening at that company that suits us perfectly."

Karen Grace Kassy, M.S., author of *Health Intuition: A Simple Guide to Greater Well-Being*, works as a health intuitive® with private clients and health care professionals from around the world.

Karen defined intuition as "knowing something without knowing how you know it." Describing how people can use their own health intuition to help themselves, she said, "I think the simplest and best thing people can do is start practicing their intuition with everyday mundane things that they don't have a big emotional stake in, like finding a parking space. Once you start on those things, you'll get better at it. Then you'll have the confidence to try bigger things."

That's how intuition works. It works in the moment, right now in the precious present. It is a prompting, a sensation, an urge to do something, say something or avoid something. Intuition often shows itself as a feeling or an inner voice which tells us to trust our spontaneity or instincts. It was intuition that prompted me to write this book. I learned many years ago to trust my intuition. My inner voice has rarely been wrong. It has been a faithful guide. When I fail to listen carefully to my intuition, I lose time, energy and direction.

In *Success, Your Dream, and You,* I wrote in my chapter on intuition, "Everyone is born with the ability to be intuitive, but often it is bred out of us as we mature. Many people think it is more "adult" to make decisions based solely on external fact, leaving out emotion. Ignoring intuition means ignoring one of the most important sources of factual information available to us. Intuition is a skill that we can practice...The more we use the process, the quicker it will occur." The more we practice it, the more adept we will become at recognizing what is true intuition and what is only wishcraft.

I can say from my own experience that my intuitive insights and hunches come regularly. They continually assist me and support my intellectual, emotional and spiritual growth. I receive guidance about what is risky and what is not, what is good for me and what to stay away from.

Gary Zukav calls this kind of guidance a *"walkie-talkie* connection between the personality and the soul." He goes on to say in his book, *The Seat of the Soul,* that "The higher self is the connecting link when the soul speaks to its human personality. It is the dialogue between the personality and its immortal self...In the creation of personality...the soul calibrates itself through the use of...intuition."

There have been many books written about intuition so it is not my intent here to belabor the subject. I've included a brief description here to reinforce its significance and promote its relevance for your own successful pathfinding adventure. Intuition is a necessary skill. If you have not developed your intuitive ability to any degree, I strongly encourage you to begin to trust your gut feelings and hunches.

Don Millman's chapter on trusting your intuition in his book, *Everyday Enlightenment*, opens with the following statement, "Below everyday awareness is a shamanlike, childlike consciousness – weaver of dreams, keeper of instinct. Your subconscious holds keys to a treasure house of intuitive wisdom, clear sight and untapped power...All you have to do is to look, listen and trust, paying attention to dreams, feelings, instinct. If you can't trust your own inner senses, what can you trust?"

One of the most interesting and enlightening guests on Positive Living was Deborah McCormick, Ph.D., co-author with her mother, Adele von Rust McCormick, of *Horse Sense and the Human Heart: What Horses Can Teach Us About Trust, Bonding, Creativity and Spirituality*. Dr. McCormick explored why horses are skillful guides, how they can help people develop their intuition, and how her work in equine therapy has rehabilitated troubled adolescents. I asked Dr. McCormick how horses teach us about intuition. She said, "They teach us how to listen to our gut feelings, how to focus on the beauty of the moment. When we are still, we begin to perceive things in the silence that we normally wouldn't. That is what horses help to do. They help us learn to be still and look inside ourselves."

She added, "You don't have to be a rider or be involved with horses to appreciate the wonder of nature. There is a whole dimension of reality that we don't pay attention to. We are so busy all the time, and are often so frantic and worried that we miss the subtle and small things that really give life a richness. The book is not just about riding. It is about how we can find our spirituality and creativity through horses and how they are the vehicle for us. They help us to get our instincts back."

To summarize the message of her book and work, Dr. McCormick said, "We as a species need to get back to interacting with nature to keep our own peace of mind and compassion. We need to remember that we are a part of creation. Reaching a state of unity with a horse reminds us of this great oneness, and these theories can apply to gardening, exercise, enjoying a favorite piece of music, writing and many others."

You can trust your *well-developed* intuitive hunches, insights and inclinations, but it takes practice. As I've said before, that's the only way to gain the confidence you need. Both your thinking and feeling natures must work in concert. Your intellectual, logical, pragmatic side must learn to release some control to your emotional, clairvoyant, creative voices. It'll take time. You'll make mistakes and sometimes you'll hear the negative and irrational voice, but once your intuitive and rational natures learn to take turns in helping you process experience, you'll discover the incredible power of your intuitive potential.

## *Search for the Hidden Gems*

*Fundamentally, when we look into our own hearts and begin to discover what is confused and what is brilliant, what is better and what is sweet, it isn't just ourselves we discover, we discover the universe.* (Ane Pema Chodron)

*B*elieve it or not, you can be your own role model if you will consistently pay attention to your gut instinct and inner voice. It sounds easy, although it can become challenging when choosing products and services that you know in your heart are right for you, but you are overruled by the voices of the world shouting at you.

The temptation to seek happiness and contentment outside of yourself is prevalent today. Advertisers entice and reward you to buy something else to make you happy. TV commercials show you thousands of things to buy, guaranteed to bring fulfillment. Add the Internet, and you have millions of opportunities to purchase happiness and success.

Newspapers and magazines bombard you with clever stories and articles that focus on your future success. Malls and shopping centers are filled with merchants whose sole purpose is to separate you from your money. The message is the same: You will not be happy unless you buy something at the places you are told to go.

How many times do you hear about a great store, therapist, book, restaurant that is not well known or advertised? It is often because the person or item hasn't been well promoted. My philosophy is to look for those people and places. They are the hidden gems and are usually not crowded or as harried as their commercial counterparts. They are often small, caring, warm and special. Some of the best professionals who have taught me the greatest lessons in life are not the famous authors and speakers. But their message is just as powerful.

Follow your own instinct when finding what you need. Big isn't always better. J.B. Priestly writes, "I have always been delighted at the prospect of a new day, a fresh try, one more start, with perhaps a bit of magic waiting somewhere behind the morning."

The truth is, you don't have to go anywhere or buy anything else to find happiness, peace and contentment. You have your own hidden gems within you. You will find them in your inner space, not the outer space of the world.

Happiness and self-satisfaction reside in your consciousness. You can only reach these treasures through introspection, focus and desire. Although they are hidden from the naked eye, they glow brightly within your spiritual eye and they are activated by your positive thoughts.

Many times the hidden gems are in your own homes, and when you get rid of what you don't need or want, you are able to uncover them. Terah Kathryn Collins, author of *The Western Guide to Feng Shui: Creating Balance, Harmony, and Prosperity in Your Environment* says, "Love what you live with, live with what you love, and express and organize yourself. The more that we can calm the human nervous system, the more we can live a serene yet very productive life."

We are all such "pack rats," saving things because of the memories attached to them, or because we think we might someday need this unused item. In her book, *Prospering Woman*, Ruth Ross states the prosperity law of releasing: "We must get rid of what we don't want to make room for what we do want." I refer to this as the law of vacuum, where the universe abhors a vacuum, immediately filling the space we've emptied. Even if we can't replace it with our ideal piece of furniture, fixture, appliance, wall covering, or collectible, we can find a hidden gem that is closer to what we truly want. For me, this has meant going through my boxes that contain memories and emptying all those drawers of accumulated stuff. What I learned during this process of shedding and releasing was to honor my past achievements, let go of what doesn't serve me anymore, and replace it with something special that meets my current needs, so that I can move in the present flow of life.

# *Pay Attention to Inner Signals to Create Balance*

*Most true happiness comes from one's inner life, from the disposition of the mind and soul. Admittedly, a good inner life is hard to achieve, especially in these trying times. It takes reflection and contemplation and self-discipline.*

(W.L. Shirer)

*C*reating balance is the way to harmony. Balance is a struggle for all of us. But in order to find balance, we must be in touch with our own needs and desires through nurturing and honoring our true selves. Sarah Ban Breathnach in her book, *Simple Abundance,* often refers to this as being authentic. And sometimes in our authenticity, we find balance by going from one extreme to the other. To avoid that roller coaster ride, you can check in with yourself every day to see where you are. Are you tired? Do your muscles ache? Are you angry? Are you overloaded with information? Do you need a kind word, reassurance or a hug? These are all signals to slow down, and take time for yourself. We are so much more effective when we pay attention, take care of what's in the way, pause, and then continue on. A simple walk outside, just breathing, talking to a friend on the phone for assurance, giving your loved ones a hug, having a sit down meal instead of eating on the run, or going to a place where you can inhale the beauty of nature may be all you need to find balance.

Balance requires listening to our inner signals as this story illustrates:

*A man and woman were strolling along a crowded sidewalk in a downtown business area. Suddenly one of them exclaimed, "Did you hear that meow?"*

*They both stopped and listened intently. "There it is again. Didn't you hear it?" asked the one who heard the kitten a second time.*

*"How can you hear that kitten's meow in this frenzied city?"*

*The companion, who was a veterinarian-turned animal rights advocate, smiled but did not explain. She simply took a quarter out of her purse and dropped it on the sidewalk, causing a dozen people to look around for the loose change.*

*"We hear," she said, "what we listen for."*

Listen for the things which bring joy and inner peace and you'll have joyous experiences. Step out on faith and you'll get faith-lifts wherever you go. According to Rabbi David Cooper, "In Judaism, the Kabalistic idea that creation is taking place in each and every moment brings an acute sensitivity to everything...an entirely new perspective that sees things as they are."

My father commented on this and said, "An example of this concept is the person with a terminal illness who has to live each moment because they can't count on future moments. This teaches all of us to live right now and do what we can now. Many times we are not satisfied with what we see. The most difficult thing to attain is satisfaction today because we always think there is something better tomorrow. It often turns out that what you wanted would not serve you as well as what you already have. You have to appreciate what you have now because there is no proof of the future. Even if you doubt your decisions based on your instincts, listen to what your heart tells you based on what

45

you know now. Set your course, stick to it and don't look back.

"For example, when you experience a medical problem, you must not panic. Read up on the medical problem facing you, for with some understanding of its nature, you are in a better position to accept or reject whatever treatment is advised."

My father continued: "One day in routinely checking our blood pressures, your mother's blood pressure was almost 200. Even though I tried to calm her down, she panicked and ran to the doctor, who gave her blood pressure pills. My advice to her was not to take those pills based on one blood pressure reading. After a few days I convinced her to go off of the pills. She has not had that high a blood pressure since."

I said to my father, "But you're also saying, pay attention, listen to yourself, get all the facts, and think of what your body is telling you."

"Well, that's true," Dad admitted. "You know, a person with terminal cancer may be told they have a year or eight months to live and that person lives a miserable eight months. On the other hand, there are people who would say, 'If that's the case, I'm going to live it up for eight months, I'm going to enjoy myself.' That person probably lives longer and lives more positively.

"At age 85-and-a-half, I am confronted with a deteriorating heart valve. The medical opinion is that I should consider surgery. The fact of the matter is no one has insisted that I definitely have the surgery. The directive to me is that I should consider having this fixed. Now, this comes at a time, when I feel pretty good for my age. I've reduced a lot of the medications I was taking, and feel better. I could also lose about 10 or 15 pounds, as I'm somewhat overweight. Yet not once did the doctor say, 'You should shed a few pounds of weight.' Isn't it logical that the less tissue for my heart to force blood through, the better? The point is you have to understand your own body well enough to help doctors do their job. And then you've got to stop worrying about it."

My father's attitude about his health makes all the difference. He recently did have the surgery, and he knows that he must contribute as much, if not more, to his own healing as health care providers. Before the surgery I asked my father if he thought he'd make it, and he responded, "Of course I do! Do you think I'd be going through this if I didn't?" After the surgery he said, "We've been given a new beginning. Let's rid ourselves of the clutter and what we don't need, and start anew."

All of the millions of words written on the subject of happiness and contentment can be reduced to two words: Know thyself. Happiness is an inside job. If we are not content on the inside, no amount of material success, pleasure or possessions will make us happy. The treasure we seek is in our own joy, balance and inner peace.

# *Seize the Power of the Moment*

> *One of the most tragic things I know about human nature is that all of us tend to put off living. We are all dreaming of some magical rose garden over the horizon–instead of enjoying the roses that are blooming outside our windows today.* (Dale Carnegie)

*T*he present moment is powerful and is all we have. Our future becomes our past in the blink of an eye. "Every second we live is a new and unique moment of the universe," says Pablo Casals. "It is a moment that never was and will never be again." Most of us live in the "now" only some of the time. In general, people are unaware of the power and joy of the present, because we keep our thoughts either in the past or on the future. My father says, "Most of us think that enjoyment lives in the future, when actually we have to learn to take the enjoyment of the moment." So often we miss the significance of the moment because our attention is cluttered with things to do next, places to be later and problems to handle tomorrow. We waste so much of our valuable time stressing over things of which we have limited personal control. As Dr. Abraham J. Twerski says in his book, *The Spiritual Self: Reflections on Recovery and God*, "Purposefulness, trust, avoiding indulgence and excess, gratitude and living one day at a time are not only noble attributes of character, but are aspects of a lifestyle that permits the attainment of joy."

Unfortunately, we generally lose ourselves in our hectic daily lives. Essential parts of us are rubbed off in the friction of the hustle and bustle nature of our out-of-control schedules. Most people are moving so fast that they are oblivious to the essential pieces of themselves – like joy, inner peace, balance, reverence and health–that are torn away by the countless collisions between now and the next moment. We have become creatures of speed.

*Many years ago, when I was living in Newburyport, on the north shore of Boston, I was driving down the street and pulled up to a traffic light. Another motorist arrived at the corner perpendicular to me at the same intersection. Although I had the right-of-way, I hesitated to pull forward because my foot was in a cast. My injury did not impair my driving, but it did make me cautious.*

*The other driver mistook my slight hesitation as permission for her to drive through the intersection. Unfortunately, I had also started through the intersection, and she hit my car. I hobbled out of my car, looked at the minor damage, and suggested that we go to the coffee shop across the street to wait for the police. She was shocked at my invitation and refused. Eventually, when we had to settle in court, she brought up my coffee invitation on the witness stand. She must have felt there was some significance or motive behind my asking her to meet and talk about the accident when in her mind we were adversaries.*

It was unfortunate that we had to go to court. No one was injured. The property damage was minor. I had tried my best to put the accident in perspective and to create a win-win situation. I was thankful no one had been hurt and wanted to turn a negative experience into a positive one by suggesting coffee. The other driver was more focused on what could have happened instead of what did happen. She missed the significance of the moment. She saw the accident as a catastrophe and missed two important lessons: the realization that both of us were okay and the assurance that all things work together for good.

This next story illustrates how staying present in the moment can save your life.

I met Rena Gelissen and Heather Dune Macadam ten years ago, when they were guests on Positive People in the Piedmont, a television talk show I hosted and produced on a Fox affiliate in North Carolina. Rena is a holocaust survivor and Heather wrote her story in the book *Rena's Promise: A Story of Sisters in Auschwitz*. Rena was on the first transport of women into Auschwitz on March 26, 1942. Her sister arrived two days later. They were freed on May 2, 1945. Together, Rena and her sister Danka, survived three years and 41 days in concentration and death camps.

My recent conversation with Heather really transformed my thinking, as she shared her perspective of how the true survival of Rena had much to do with staying in the present moment.

*Heather said, "I do believe that part of Rena's survival mechanism was just truly to stay in the present. She told me that at one point the girls from the city, who were in the camp with her, were still busy thinking about when they had been pretty and had nail polish on. They were so stunned and shocked at the transformation that occurred – to lose everything and to all of the sudden be slaves, to be shaved, and to have horribly lice ridden clothes, that they kept going back to who they had been before. Many of them lost their minds or didn't make it."*

Heather went on to recount a powerful story of how Rena saved her own life:

50

*I feel that the reason that Rena was able to escape from Dr. Mengele's brutal and fatal experiments was that she stayed in the present, observing what was happening around them and assessing it quickly. Rena was standing in line with her sister in nicely ironed dresses with aprons on, and as she was standing there, she saw the person in charge sneak one of the girls out of line and take her behind a building. She knew immediately that this was not a work detail but that 'this was a detail for death.' Why else would the person in charge sneak a prisoner – who might have been a sister, or cousin,*

*If Rena had been standing there thinking about her parents, or what her life had been like before freedom – she would not have recognized the danger they were in, or been able to act on it.*

*She took her sister's hand and told her, 'We have to go back to where our old uniforms are, get them on and sneak into line in roll call without getting caught.'*

*Frightened by the enormity and danger of this proposal, her sister responded that she cannot do it. However, Rena reminded her – once again – stay rooted in reality and use reality as a way to act – we're going to die anyway. Her logic was pure Auschwitz logic – you can die whether or not you try and live – so why not try and live?*

*They had absolutely nothing to lose. Rena took her sister's hand and said "Danka, we're invisible. Take my hand and hold up your chin high.' And they walked across camp as if they had been ordered to. Nobody stopped them. Nobody questioned them. Rena found their old clothes with their prisoner numbers on them, got them dressed and snuck them back into roll call without anyone noticing their escape from Mengele's detail, and they were alive.*

If staying in the present moment can literally save your life, what more can it do in less severe situations? When I was selecting stories for this chapter, I chose ones that illustrated how staying in the present allows us to truly enjoy the moments we have and savor them. Heather's account is so powerful and visceral and she really captured Rena's important, historical story. It wasn't until this story that I connected with the theory that staying in the moment is also a strong survival mechanism. When you are truly able to receive your joy from staying in the present, you can use this positive discipline to keep you in the present and move forward during times of sorrow or life threatening situations.

Staying in the present moment and paying attention means realizing that each moment, every minute, each hour and every day is important and has significance. The following is my recollection of a story I heard Dr. Leo Buscaglia tell many years ago that has stayed with me.

*A woman who heard Dr. Buscaglia speak at a conference was so touched by his message that she pleaded with him to come to her house, which was right around the corner from the conference facility. Even though Dr. Buscaglia was operating a tight time schedule, he agreed to go for a few minutes. When she introduced Dr. Buscaglia to her husband. Before the men could speak, she launched a barrage of questions intended to make the good doctor comfortable: "Dr. Buscaglia, may I get you some water? May I get you some coffee or tea? Would you like something to eat? Your presentation was so wonderful...I couldn't believe...I had no idea...Will you sign my book?"*

*She was so focused on the trivial that she missed the vital few minutes she could have enjoyed with Dr. Buscaglia. Her constant chatter turned a precious moment into a lost moment, and she missed what could have been a positive, life-enriching experience.*

This can happen when we feel rushed and overburdened, overwhelmed with job responsibilities and family obligations, pressured by time and constrained by our ability to juggle ten things at once. We then fail to see the connection between what we're doing, what we're meant to do and what we can do. We miss opportunities for clarity and direction, and we forget the very things that can help us find balance and gain the perspective we need to value each moment.

When you search for moments of joy, inner peace and balance, you will attract activities, work, hobbies, conversations, people and circumstances that bring joy, inner peace and balance into your life. Focusing on what you want, brings you the essence of what you want.

By seizing the power of the moment myself recently, I gained a lifetime memory as well as validation of my work.

*My husband and I recently went to see the famous musical "Fiddler on the Roof" about Jewish family tradition at the turn of the century. I hadn't seen the musical in many years but remembered all the songs, and sang along softly to myself. The story was so close to my heart, covering the unrest of the day I know my grandfather experienced in Russia, the father-daughter relationship that I relate to with my father and the orthodox traditions and rituals that my orthodox brother and his family practice today. I was really so touched by the performances, especially of Theodore Bikel, who played the lead role of Tevye. Mr. Bikel, now in his late seventies, played the role for many years when "Fiddler on the Roof" was on Broadway.*

*After the show, I had this burning desire to meet Theodore Bikel and get his autograph. Seeing how*

*moved I was by the performance, my husband encour-
aged me to do it, for which I am very grateful. On the
way out of the theatre, the woman who played Golde,
wife of Tevye, was standing at the door collecting
donations for a children's charity. I asked her if she
thought I could get an autograph and she told me that
if I went to the stage door, someone would perhaps
take my program to Mr. Bikel for a signature. We got
very confusing directions to the stage door, and discovered there were several doors. We tried the doors
we found and none opened. The last direction we got
was to a door that was up a little hill. Just as we were
walking up, there was Theodore Bikel getting into a
car! He was surrounded by an entourage of five people. My husband said to me, "There he is. You've got
to talk with him." We were on the right side of the car
and I asked the woman standing there if Mr. Bikel
would give me an autograph. She looked at the others
on the other side of the car where he had just been
seated, and they motioned me to go over to him.
Theodore Bikel was gracious and kind. I told him how
much the performance meant to me and about the
book I am writing with my 85 year-old Jewish father.
He signed my playbill and then looked right into my
eyes with a smile. It was so powerful and went right
through me. I felt like I was looking into the eyes of a
wise sage and I could feel all those seasoned years of
experience and wisdom. I took advantage of the
moment, which took some persistence, but I got to
meet Theodore Bikel, whose presence up close and in
person was just so awesome.*

The timeless relevance of each precious moment reminds
us: "To everything there is a season, and a time to every purpose under the heaven; A time to be born, and a time to die;

A time to plant, and a time to pluck up that which is planted; A time to kill, and a time to heal; A time to break down, and a time to build up; A time to weep, and a time to laugh; A time to mourn, and a time to dance; A time to cast away stones, and a time to gather stones together; A time to embrace, and a time to refrain from embracing; A time to get, and a time to lose; A time to keep, and a time to cast away; A time to rend, and a time to sew; A time to keep silence, and a time to speak; A time to love, and a time to hate; A time of war, and a time of peace." (Ecclesiastes 3:1-8)

The writer of Ecclesiastes placed a value on everything we do. Each moment has a purpose and holds a significant place in our development. Living today is the most basic building block for tomorrow. This concept is most vivid for me in raising our children. I often look at my daughter's childhood pictures as the building blocks of her life. The memories are captured in the pictures where I can retrieve those moments in my heart and mind. But in physical reality, those moments are gone. We can really appreciate them in the "here and now" when we become a permanent resident of the present. Don't underestimate the power of the moment.

"Stop to smell the roses," as the saying goes. Spend time with loved ones. Say "I love you" often. Don't let a day go by without telling people dear to you how much they mean to you. Stop long enough to hear the chorus of birds on your way to work. Notice how golden the sun is. Give your child, your spouse, a family member an extra-long hug. Eat your food and sip your coffee or tea instead of inhaling it. Appreciate the texture, color, taste and aroma. Examine the petals of a flower. Study one of your favorite pictures or paintings. Pay attention to how you are sitting. Notice how you greet and meet people. Close your eyes and listen to the sounds of nature outside.

A guest on Positive Living, Dr. J. T. Garrett, member of the Eastern Band of Cherokee Indians, and author of *Medicine of the Cherokee: The Way Of Right Relationship,* shared what his grandfather taught him about how nature teaches us to stay in the present: "My grandfather was very clear and funny in a lot of things that he would say and do, and he made it enjoyable. Instead of being a strict teacher telling us which way to do something, he would just get us involved in doing things in nature, like searching for the special rock. We often forget about being a child and what it's like to be able to play for hours with nothing, no special toys, no Tonkas, no whatever the current game is, and instead get out in nature and enjoy little things."

I encourage you to develop a "now" mentality. Practice in-the-moment living. Because each moment becomes your life passage, history and legacy combined, it makes good sense to be fully aware of how each moment affects you. "Only by living consciously in the present," says G. W. Casper, "can we grasp the full meaning of our lives."

## *Give Thanks For Your Blessings*

*Gratitude unlocks the fullness of life. It turns what we have into enough, and more. It turns denial into acceptance, chaos into order, confusion into clarity. It can turn a meal into a feast, a house into a home, a stranger into a friend. Gratitude makes sense of our past, brings peace for today, and creates a vision for tomorrow.* (Melody Beattie)

*T*he special positive moments in our lives only happen once. They are snapshots in time. Those moments bring us love and comfort in our moments of fear, despair, loneliness and pain. They are always with us and we use them to create, weave and spin our memories together. When you imprint them in your mind, like an affirmation, you are creating a blueprint of what you want in your daily life. So think and talk about those precious moments and be grateful for them. Count your blessings. It brings you many more.

Giving thanks is a precondition for positive living. It is one of the chief ingredients for our maturation and growth. We need a dose of it every day to fortify us from grief caused by lack of appreciation and self-centeredness. Unfortunately, we can't take a pill for ingratitude or a vaccination to protect ourselves from complacency or selfishness. Thanksgiving is an attitude, and attitudes spring from the beliefs and values that filter those attitudes.

During my interview with Dr. Garrett, right before Thanksgiving, I asked him for some closing thoughts to us as we approached this holiday. Dr. Garrett said, "Our goal should be to say thank you every day. It is difficult to be angry at somebody when you are smiling, and it is also difficult to be angry at the world when you are giving thanks."

Sarah Ban Breathnach in her bestselling book, *Simple Abundance: A Daybook of Comfort and Joy*, takes this one step further and urges us to use a gratitude journal. She writes: "The gratitude journal has to be the first step on the Simple Abundance path or it just won't work for you. Simplicity, order, harmony, beauty and joy – all the other principles that can transform your life will not blossom and flourish without gratitude. If you want to travel this journey with me, the gratitude journal is not an option. Why? Because you simply will not be the same person two months from now after consciously giving thanks each day for the abundance that exists in your life, And you will have set in motion an ancient spiritual law; the more you have and are grateful for, the more will be given you."

The incomprehensible terrorist attacks on the World Trade Center on September 11th remind us vividly of the need to savor each precious moment. If there is one lesson I carry with me from what happened on that day, it's to count and appreciate my blessings today, right now, this minute. Dr. Mark Williams, a guest on my show (whom you will hear more from in Chapter 5) told me that when he leaves his house and kisses his wife good-bye, he never takes it for granted that he will see her again and knows that it could be the last time they are together. If we felt that way more often, we would make moments more meaningful. We would argue less, fret less, be angry less, be more grateful and more joyful.

I left my house that fateful morning before I heard the news. I was agitated because I was about twenty minutes late for a meeting. But my agitation suddenly turned to gratefulness, because we had just gotten back from vacation and could have easily been on one of those planes. My daughter just moved to New York City, luckily on the other side of the city, nowhere near the twin towers. I am still haunted by the implications of September 11th. What happened to those innocent people could have happened to any of us. None of us are promised tomorrow.

Whatever it takes, do something today that you've been putting off. Call your family and tell them you love them. Do what you've been wanting to do but have put off. Pray for the thousands of people affected by the abominable events of September 11th. Pray to God, because God is there. There is too much beauty in our world and too many good people for God not to be there.

I'd like to share another personal story with you, about a man who really knew how to live in the now and squeeze every bit out of life. His name was Mel Goldberg, and he was a good friend of my father whose first name is also Mel.

*My father and Mel, who was a writer and medical publisher, commuted for several years to New York City together from Stamford, Connecticut.*

*During a time when I was caring for my parent's home while they were away, I had the opportunity to spend time with Mel and his wife, Louise, who lived a street away. When Louise died suddenly in a car accident, I was able to be there for him. He was instrumental in helping me write my first book. We used to walk, bike and swim together. When I moved out of the area, I stayed in touch with Mel. And I'm so glad I did.*

*One evening Mel called Antonio and me to announce his plans to vacation in the Galapagos Islands. He and his companion, Joan, were "going on a well-deserved vacation," he said. This was the last time I spoke with him. He suffered a fatal heart attack while he and Joan were snorkeling.*

*The man who shared the same first name as my father; who was so supportive in helping me get my first book published; who rode with my father to New York City for years; whose favorite phrase about my father was, "I would ride to New York and listen to the wit and wisdom of Mel Raskin," the man who called me "kiddo" – was gone! I can't tell you how shocked we were with the news of his death.*

*He was taken from us in an instant, but as Joan so eloquently put it, "Mel died in a beautiful place. He didn't suffer. He didn't have Alzheimer's or any other disease that he feared so much. He didn't want to be a burden."*

*Joan continued, "I sensed from Mel's behavior before he passed away, that he was winding up his life, in spite of the fact that he was very healthy. There was no sensible reason why he thought he would be passing away soon. He put all his affairs in order to the extent that I commented to a couple of friends of ours how unusual this was. I have to feel that on some level he knew he didn't have long."*

Mel squeezed every ounce out of life. He had a child-like fascination and zest for everything he did and he truly loved life. Mel was such a generous man, always lending a helping hand to family, friends and those in need. I think Mel's message would have been, 'love deeply, live fully, give to others and appreciate your life.' Mel died the way he lived, doing something he loved, surrounded by beauty.

I feel fortunate that I have my own Mel – my father – whom I love dearly. Antonio and I try to spend as much time as we can with my parents. They've been married over 58 years now, and I feel so blessed to have them. And like Mel Goldberg said, I plan to enjoy the "wit and wisdom of Mel Raskin" for a long time.

## *Turn Up Your Laughter Meter*

> *There is a form of laughter that springs from the heart, which has nothing rigid or mechanical in it. It bubbles spontaneously from the heart of child or man. It is without egotism and full of feeling. Laughter is the music of life.*
> (Sir William Osler)

*J*oel Goodman, Director of the HUMOR Project, Inc., in Saratoga Springs, New York, the first organization in the world to focus full-time on the positive power of humor, and author of *Laffirmations: 1001 Ways to Add Humor to Your Life and Work*, said on my radio program, "With change all around us, if you're not mentally flexible, if you're not able to roll with the punches that life throws at you, you'll be more easily knocked off balance. Humor is a great way of helping us keep our balance, keep our perspective, keep our creativity and keep on going."

Also on the program was career coach Bobbi Gemma, who has been doing humor training for ten years. She said, "For me, it all boils down to my father's philosophy of life which is: 'If you're going to go, you might as well have a good time. If you're going to do it, you might as well enjoy it.' If we apply that to all aspects of our lives, it makes everything flow better, it helps us relate better, be more productive, and maintain our health, sanity, stability and probably longevity."

The late Terry Barts, a remarkably inspirational youth pastor, said on my program, "Every time I look in the mirror, I am reminded that God has a sense of humor. A youngster told me recently that God made all the animals except the camel and He allowed a committee to make that one. That's why I stay with young people. They'll laugh at you so you might as well laugh at yourself. A lot of people have forgotten how to laugh and how to see things from a child's perspective."

I talk about laughter and healing in *Success, Your Dream and You:* "Laughter is a powerful form of healing. Physiologically, laughter deepens breathing, strengthens the immune system and massages the internal organs. Laughter offers a form of detachment and relief from our own situations. Laughter also stimulates the thymus gland which protects the immune system, becoming a source of illness prevention. Laughter stimulates deep breathing, helps us 'save face,' and deal with difficult people. It brings 'lightness' into our lives, transforms bad moods into good moods, and adds joy and fun to our lives."

It's fun and uplifting to be around people who have a healthy sense of humor, because they have an active "laughter meter," they enjoy life. In fact, when I think of some of the spirited conversations I've had with them, I picture all of us laughing and having a good time. Laughter is therapeutic. There's something about it that's extremely healing.

I love Carol Channing's quote about laughter, when she said, "Laughter is much more important than applause. Applause is almost considered a duty, laughter is a reward." When you start to wind down your day and discover you haven't laughed very much, do something that makes you laugh. If it's been a tiresome day, or a troublesome one, you have to work harder for your laughter. But laugh you must! A couple of doses of laughter will help you feel both physically and emotionally lighter.

As I mentioned before, Joel Goodman's book *Laffirmations: 1001 Ways to Add Humor to Your Life and Work* puts laughter in perspective. Mr. Goodman writes: "Humor is important, jest for the health of it! Perhaps the most significant bottom line is your health – without it, you're dead (literally or figuratively). Norman's best-selling book, *Anatomy of an Illness,* certainly opened many people's eyes to the notion that "people who laugh last." William Fry, Jr., M.D., who has done research on the physiology of laughter for forty-five years, lends support to Norman's notion that laughter is like "internal jogging." Laughter enhances respiration and circulation, oxygenates the blood, suppresses the stress-related hormones in the brain, and activates the immune system. Indeed laughter is "jest the medicine."

On Positive Living with Joel Goodman and Bobbi Gemma, Mr. Goodman gave this homework assignment. "For five minutes a day," says Goodman, "make believe you're Allen Funt, the guy who hosted the Candid Camera show on TV. The premise of that show was that if we catch people in the act of being themselves, laughter is on its way. All we have to do is to look for humor. So for five minutes, take a mental time out and look for the humor around you. It's there, present, alive and well, just waiting to be seen." Bobbi Gemma added, "I think it's a matter of practice. It's like stretching a muscle. I tell groups that every one of us has enough humor around us to create a ten-minute stand-up routine. Once you find your ten minutes of humor, the next challenge is to share it with other people. When you share it, it magnifies and grows."

The sounds of laughter are the sounds of fun and enjoyment. It's a natural endorphin rush. It's the body's way of saying, "Take care of yourself. Stop taking everything so seriously. Relax, and most of all, enjoy life."

# *Positive Pollination*

*List:*
- ❖ Five things in your life you are thankful for.
- ❖ A solution that you "know" intuitively (without thinking).
- ❖ Special moments from your life that are "snapshots in time."
- ❖ People, places and things that bring you laughter.

*Reflect on:*
- ❖ How your intuition has helped you make the right decisions.
- ❖ How often you give thanks.
- ❖ How being grateful has brought you more abundance.
- ❖ How staying in the present moment has helped you avert danger.
- ❖ How staying in the present moment has brought you immense joy.

# CHAPTER THREE

# Use Your
# Imperfections to
# Perfect Your Life

*As they traveled in the Land of Oz, the quick-witted scarecrow thought he had no brains; the loving tin woodsman felt he needed a heart; and the heroic lion believed he lacked courage.*

(Frank L. Baum)

*N*obody's perfect! How many times have you heard that expression? Many people use it as an excuse to justify their well-practiced inadequacies. Others use it to excuse their inability to achieve certain goals. Some people, however, use it as a standard excuse. Quite a few use it to excuse someone's failure. And there are some who use it, all too frequently, to avoid any kind of self-improvement.

Is anyone perfect? I believe we are perfectly imperfect. There are parts of us that need improvement and there are parts of us that are pretty much okay. Perfect imperfection means we are exactly where we are supposed to be, given our limitations. Anais Nim wrote about perfect imperfection, "Every one of us carries a deforming mirror where we see ourselves too small or too large, too fat or too thin. We discover that destiny can be directed, that we do not need to remain in bondage to the first imprint made on childhood sensibilities, we need not be branded by the first pattern. Once the deforming mirror is smashed, there is the possibility of wholeness and joy."

Self-discovery is an indispensable outcome in all pathfinding. I have come to realize that our journey toward selfhood is not so much self-*discovery* as it is self-*recovery*. We recover parts of us that have been dormant, repressed, inhibited or forgotten. Serious attempts at pathfinding help us revive those hidden parts of us that have been distorted by events in our lives that have impacted us.

Most of us, at one time or another, adopt attitudes and behaviors that reinforce our limitations and hold us back. We focus on our imperfections instead of the things we do well. We berate ourselves when we make mistakes or fail at something. Many people tolerate poor treatment and stay in debilitating relationships because they believe they cannot or do not deserve better. Too many people use illnesses, injuries and health challenges as excuse devices to give up on themselves. Drs. Harold Bloomfield and Robert Kory, co-authors of the best-selling *TM: Discovering Inner Energy and Overcoming Stress* and *The Holistic Way to Health and Happiness* refer to these deforming mirrors as "self-canceling acts."

Because I strive to see things in a positive light, I believe we can use our imperfections to perfect our lives. I have found this to be true in my own pathfinding. The key to clearing up the distorting mirrors is to love yourself enough, in spite of your imperfections, to give yourself a chance at becoming the person you can be. You must take full advantage of what you do well by staying positive, affirming your self-worth and adopting life-enriching attitudes that amplify your strengths.

## *Love Yourself, Warts and All*

*We are born broken. We live by mending. The*
*grace of God is the glue.*     (Eugene O'Neill)

*S*elf-acceptance is a full time job. It is the greater part
of self-fulfillment and a necessary part of our growth
and development. Accepting ourselves for who we are and
why we are is our fundamental calling. Some of us are
beautiful, tall and athletic. Others are comely, short and able
bodied, but not necessarily athletic. Most of us have had
pimples, warts, freckles, sties or moles, birthmarks and
minor deformities. People have birth defects, blotches,
spots, specks, creases, wrinkles, dimples, blisters and bruises. All of us have cuts, scrapes, blemishes and scars. Some
of us have health challenges, others have serious life-threat-
ening health difficulties. People have physical, mental and
emotional impairments. We all have faults, inadequacies,
weaknesses, shortcomings, vulnerabilities and Achilles'
heels.

Despite all of our imperfections, we find ourselves sur-
prisingly alike. Rabbi Ted Falcon puts it this way, "We are
not so different from all the peoples of this world, yet the
message which has come through us is special and unique.
To discover, express and expand our uniqueness, as individuals, and as a people, supports 'tikkun ha-olam,' the
completion of creation, to which we are called. With grati-

tude, then, we reach into the heart of our uniqueness. Not to best another, but to better understand ourselves."

I believe the rabbi has a point here. Perhaps the disappointments and suffering we experience in our uniqueness as human beings has to do with the completion of creation.

Suppose our imperfections are part of the perfect plan for our lives? That would explain why some people have warts and others have beauty marks. It would shed light on why some people have wrinkles and others have dimples. It could answer why some people seem to attract health difficulties and others suffer emotional impairments. It could answer the questions Rabbi Harold Kushner asks in his book, *When Bad Things Happen to Good People*: "Why do righteous people suffer? Why do good people have to go through so much pain? Why do bad things happen to good people?"

These are universal questions to which there may not be a satisfactory answer. Many wise people have attempted to put our vulnerabilities, suffering and warts in perspective. My pathfinding has led me to this conclusion: Our uniqueness puts us in a perfect position to turn hardships, handicaps and disabilities into catalysts for our own growth and greatness in an imperfect world.

My very dear friend, Joan-Ellen Foyder wrote *The Family Caregiver's Guide* as a way to cope with her mother's illness. She shows us how to keep track of medications, the patient's activities and our own feelings. Joan-Ellen was a true advocate, not only for caregivers, but for patients' independence and mobility. She was the spokesperson for several companies that produced assistive devices, and showed patients and caregivers on national television how to use tools to open jars, cut things, take a bath alone, dress themselves with attractive special-made clothing, and do many other things independently. Joan-Ellen was a pioneer, crusading for patients and caregivers before this way of thinking became part of the mainstream. She died several years ago of breast cancer. Her death has been a great loss to me, not just because of what she stood for, but because her commitment to care giving encouraged me to remain committed to directing and producing my Positive Living show.

Van Ekeren, author of *12 Simple Secrets of Happiness* gives his perspective as previous director of People Development for Village Northwest Unlimited, an organization dedicated to meeting the needs of people with disabilities. When I interviewed him on my radio program, he said, "In twenty years of working with people with disabilities, what I experienced the most was their undying perseverance to enjoy every day. They had a passion for life that was undeniable. I learned from them that what's important is for us to set the expectations of what our life should be. We should not allow other people to determine what those expectations are. I learned never to let anyone, anything or any experience determine the quality of my life."

The author of *12 Simple Secrets of Happiness* makes several important points. Some of the basic conditions of growth are self-acceptance, perseverance and a passion for expressing who we are regardless of the expectations or opinions of others. In many cases, the person with the greater disability is not the one with the actual physical limitation, but the one who refuses to accept it.

According to Glen Van Ekeren, "A question that we all need to ask ourselves since some of our disabilities aren't as visible as others is, 'How much could I do if I didn't know how much I could do? What other things would I try if I hadn't already established the limitations on what I think I can do?' There's a whole world of experiences out there if we will take the risk to see what else life has to offer. It's really fun to watch people break out of their boxes, so to speak, their self-imposed limitations and other-imposed limitations."

Judith Sherven, Ph.D and James Sniechowski, Ph.D., are a husband and wife psychology team and authors of *Be Loved for Who You Really Are* and *The New Intimacy.* When they were guests on my radio program, Dr. Sherven said, "When love is present in a relationship, love moves a sense of unlovability to the surface, because even though we may believe we are unlovable, we don't want to admit it. When love is present, that which has not been loved, mocked or ridiculed in the other person will surface. Relationships that have their feet on the ground enhance the healing process because the shared love will insist on it." Dr. Sniechowski added, "Love does not love just the pretty parts, love loves the entire being, warts included. And if the warts need healing then love welcomes them to the surface."

When you accept yourself, warts and all, anything is possible. Accepting your own imperfections also means accepting the world's imperfections. A guest on my program, Gail Straub, author of *The Rhythm of Compassion: Caring for Self, Connecting With Society,* discussed the importance of understanding ourselves and then serving society. She said, "Be brave, start small, do something that you enjoy and don't over commit. That is a treasure of a little phrase to remember, because it says you can't go toward an arena of suffering that you are not ready for. If you go beyond what's authentic, or too far out of your comfort zone, you won't be as skillful or able to contribute as much. But on the other side, it is really amazing how much our hearts can bear. If you take it slowly, respecting your unique internal rhythm of compassion, your heart grows bigger and deeper, and then at a certain moment, what you weren't ready for a year or two years ago, you are now ready to do. Then it is very meaningful and very enriching. It's not something that scares you and causes you to contract. It actually enriches you and makes you a better person."

The fears we face, the obstacles we encounter, the disabilities we incur, and the disappointments we suffer are all *warts* on our path to personhood. Do not be disheartened by your imperfections. Remove, modify or conceal the ones you can. Have the courage to accept the ones you can't. Decide how much of *you* would be lost without your imperfections.

I vividly remember a woman I was interviewing when I began my "positive media" journey in the earliest days of cable television programming. Her body was covered with burn scars from a horrible childhood accident. This woman was married to a business leader in the community. When I visited her home, she was wearing shorts and a sleeveless shirt. What struck me was her absolute comfort in exposing her burns. She spoke with such confidence and poise, as she talked about her infant son, to whom she had played classical music during her pregnancy and throughout his infancy. She was so committed to her child's development that after a while I didn't even see the scars. I was completely immersed in her energy and enthusiasm.

Michelangelo carved David from a flawed block of marble. Another sculptor had begun work on the block and then abandoned it when he discovered a flaw. A deep gash in the side of the block made the stone "unacceptable" to sculptors for decades. Michelangelo, however, saw something in the marble that no one else saw. He accepted the marble, warts and all, and created a masterpiece.

Barbra Streisand refused surgery on her nose. Mel Tillis sings to hide his stutter. Jimmy Durante kept his snozola. Bing Crosby exposed his ears. Michael J. Fox continues to act despite his battle with Parkinson's disease. All of these people have one thing in common: they turned their warts into wands. And so can you.

# *Let Your Inner Strength Guide You*

*Transformation comes from looking deeply within, to a state that exists before fear and isolation arise, the state in which we are inviolably whole just as we are. We connect to ourselves, to our own true experience, and discover that to be alive means to be whole.* (Sharon Salzberg)

*W*e all have strengths and weaknesses. We can use our strengths to overcome our weaknesses when we believe in and follow our own inner guidance. We don't give ourselves enough credit. Our bodies and minds know instinctively what part of us needs help and we have the resources to get what we need to compensate for what we lack. People who understand the importance of personal development know that a high degree of inner strength is necessary to help them meet the challenges associated with 21st Century living.

As my father has so wisely reminded me, using inner strength to compensate for physical weakness is not a new concept. It is as old as man himself. My father uses the biblical story of David and Goliath to illustrate the power of mental muscle over physical might."

*David was a shepherd when the Jews lived in the land of the Philistines. They had a giant called Goliath, a huge, towering nine-foot gladiator who challenged the Israelites to battle. The Philistine army and the Israeli army were facing each other when Goliath came forward. He said he would fight the best Israelite. The two gladiators would fight it out and decide the outcome of the war. The Israelites didn't have a champion to match Goliath.*

*As they considered what they should do, a shepherd boy, David, volunteered to fight Goliath. The Israelis discounted him at first. They told him that Goliath was three times his size and ten times his strength. But David persisted and the Israelites, out of desperation, let him go to do battle with Goliath. David refused body armor because of its weight and constricting effect. Nevertheless, he confronted Goliath in the field of battle.*

*David, the shepherd boy, had only his trusted slingshot. Goliath was clad in extensive protective body armor and armed to the teeth. As Goliath approached David to destroy him, David put a rock in his slingshot and waited patiently. David aimed at the only vulnerable spot the giant left exposed. He hit Goliath right between the eyes and killed him instantly.*

The Israelites faced a mountain of a man who presented a mountain of a challenge. Drawing from his inner strength, David saw the massive obstacle for what it was – a flawed problem which could be solved with surgical insight.

Instead of seeing the problem as insurmountable, David relied on his inner wisdom and the knowledge that in God all things are possible. David met the challenge head-on with the confidence and poise one gets by allowing his inner strength to guide him.

It's a wonderful lesson for all of us. David knew that fear is something he must face and overcome, not something to run from. Eleanor Roosevelt said, "You gain strength, courage and confidence by every experience in which you stop to look fear in the face. You are able to say to yourself, 'I lived through this horror. I can handle the next thing that comes along.' You must do the thing you think you cannot do."

Every fear you experience, each perceived danger, and every doubt you manufacture does not come from the *outside*, but from your own belief system. And your belief system is based on the strengths and weaknesses of your thinking. When you sweep negativity from your consciousness, you will have come a long way toward establishing an inner foundation based on strength, faith and confidence.

It is our inner vision which sustains us through any trial or uncertainty. The following story about a man who used his inner strength to overcome a disability illustrates the power of our inner vision.

Bill Irwin, author of *Blind Courage*, was the first blind person to hike the 2,100-mile Appalachian Trail from the mountains of Georgia to the mountains of Maine. His only companion was his devoted dog, Orient. When I interviewed Bill on my television program, Positive People in the Piedmont several years ago, he talked about the difficult times he faced as he stumbled over rocks, weathered the cold, and wandered off the trail. Bill's only guides were Orient, other hikers and his own well-developed sense of direction.

It would take great courage for those of us who have our sight to make this very long trek from Georgia to Maine.

Bill had a quiet strength about him as he sat in the chair next to me with his dog, Orient at his feet. In his book he writes:

*"Ten miles was an insignificant part of the two thousand miles it would take me to complete the trip, but if I strung together enough ten-mile days, I'd get from one end of the trail to the other. Consistency and time were the keys."*

Bill also had a strong faith in God and he believed it was this faith which gave him the courage to walk the trail:

*"I walked God's trail for only two of my fifty years. My conversion experience was still fresh in my mind. There was still a long way to go, but I could say a big prayer of thanks every time I looked back at where I'd been...I realized, I could have done it another way, another trail, another route, or maybe something entirely different. I could have done anything I wanted. The A.T. (Appalachian Trail) was truly a vehicle. It was there to facilitate events that would never otherwise have happened. It took some of the events along the way, some of the hardships, some of the solitude, to bring out the real me. The Trail forced me to deal with things I'd never bothered to deal with before."*

*I recently interviewed Bill again after 10 years. He shared that no blind person before or since him has made the thru-hike on the Appalachian Trail. It took him 8 1/2-months, which was 258 days. Bill now gives motivational talks all over the country, is still involved with the hiking community on the Appalachian Trail and enjoys cycling. I said to him, "Being blind hasn't stopped you at all." He responded, "No, just slowed me down a little bit doing some things."*

*I also asked if his other senses are more developed because he doesn't have sight. He said, "I do pay more attention to the other senses than most people do. I was one of the participants in a study done at Duke University about 11 years ago that showed the correlation between deafness and blindness. Most people say, 'You can hear so much better than normal people.' Well, it's not true. In fact, most blind people also have hearing loss. but it appears we hear better because we are more focused. It's what you pay attention to that really counts."*

*I asked Bill if there was a blessing in his blindness and he said, "Without the blindness, my whole life would have taken a completely different turn. I might have hiked the Appalachian Trail, but it wouldn't have had nearly the impact that it has had, simply because people perceive it as being impossible."*

*On being disabled, Bill said, "I don't think that anyone is disabled unless they're in a coma. Most of us who have disabilities are just 'differently abled.' My wife and I are building a house and people told us that it was impossible for a blind person to build a house without professional help. We are now constructing the roof and we've had absolutely no professional help at all. We did the footings for the foundations, handled logs that weigh anywhere from twelve hundred to two thousand pounds and we've done every bit of it ourselves. But because we are highly motivated, we just set our minds to do it regardless. I believe that anybody can do anything they want to do if they want to do it badly enough. So I say to people, if I can do it, anyone can do it. That's the literal fact."*

*For those people who aren't "differently-abled" Bill said, "And that goes for them too. I think we are*

76

*all encumbered by some kind of hang up. So whether it's physical or mental makes no difference. To get beyond that we have to get outside ourselves and tune into strength. Mine happens to be God." A quote by John Watson sums it up, "Be kind, for everyone you meet is fighting a battle."*

Another guest on my radio program with Bill Irwin was Tom Whittaker, author of *Higher Purpose*, the heroic story of the first disabled man to conquer Everest.

*Tom had been a mountain climber before an auto accident which resulted in his right foot being amputated and kneecap removed. In 1981 Tom founded The Cooperative Wilderness Handicap Outdoor Group (The HOG's), an organization that works with the disabled in the wilderness as physical and emotional therapy and helps them envision the future and their dreams. He said, "This was one of three or four organizations at the time that helped to find the capabilities of people with disabilities through recreation. It put the locus of control totally in their hands and showed them how jump right back up and go back to their sport as soon as they could. This kind of passion to become world class at what they were doing, was what I wanted to instill in people."*

*Tom talked about how this experience has made him a better person and said, "One of the good things about hitting bottom is that you've got something solid to push off from. I had to reinvent, redefine and reevaluate who Tom Whittaker was. Before you can reevaluate and redefine yourself, you have to be able to define who you were, what your values were and what was important to you. Then you have to work with these truths to develop the new, better person that you want to become. I think it put me much more in touch with my spirituality and helped me to understand that it is not what I can get, but what I can give. It made me a more compassionate, less self-absorbed, more focused individual. I think that's true for most people who have overcome some very large obstacle in life. We all have our Everest to climb and for me, Everest became a very literal allegory."*

*Tom's advice on going for your dream is, "Never ever give up on your dreams no matter how impractical or unrealistic you dream is. After the accident, I was lying broken in a hospital bed with oozing bandages on my right foot, broken to the knees with irreparable damage and multiple fractures of both legs, broken ribs and a crushed clavicle. If I had told people at that time that I was going to get out of that hospital bed and someday stand on the summit of Mount Everest, they would have put me in a straight jacket and shut me in a padded cell where I couldn't do myself any harm! We tend to set goals for ourselves that meet other people's expectations. I think we have to set our goals based on what gives us the most pleasure, the most joy and the most personal growth. For me, it was working with other people in wild environments and especially in high places. The vertical challenge of rock climbing, led me to climb my own Mount Everest."*

Recently CNN's Larry King interviewed Mattie Stepanek, an 11-year-old best-selling poet who has a rare form of muscular dystrophy. He lost three other siblings to this disease, and his mother recently acquired an adult onset of muscular dystrophy. With all of that, Mattie is making his dream to be an ambassador of peace come true. He shared excerpts from his best-selling book of poems *Hope Through*

*Heartsongs.* Here is a young man who is on constant life support, and doesn't know if he'll live another day; yet he not only speaks with intelligence, grace and empathy, but is also filled with hope. I was so touched by this extraordinary interview, and kept thinking about the power of Mattie's message. Then it struck me that he is able to share his message, and we listen, because of the body he has been given. I don't think we would listen as carefully if Mattie came in a "normal package." He is a true example of using strength to overcome weakness.

## *Transform Obstacles Into Opportunities*

> *There are two ways of meeting difficulties: you alter the difficulties or you alter yourself to meet them.* (Phyllis Bottome)

*S*et-backs, disappointments and tragedies often require us to come up with new, sometimes revolutionary, solutions because the old, traditional approaches are no longer viable. These life-changing detours force us to reconsider our steps, sometimes to the extent that we have to reinvent ourselves. The following stories are the accounts of men and women who have used their courage and bravery and drawn on their inner resources to create fulfilling lives for themselves. Somewhere, they saw a glimmer of light and started moving toward it.

*The first story is about my husband, Antonio. At the age of seventeen, his family fled Castro's Cuba. His father had been a prominent pediatric surgeon in Cuba and lived a very comfortable lifestyle with his family. They lost everything when they left the country. It took his father, in his mid-fifties, seven years to learn English and get a medical license in the United States.*

*Antonio helped support his family when they first came here and put himself through school. He went on to college, medical school and residency. After fourteen years of training, he became a plastic surgeon. When I shared what I wrote with Antonio, he responded, "I feel very fortunate that I was given the opportunity to excel and that I was able to take advantage of the doors that were open to me. It was no easy task because I had to relearn everything and then replace my culture with a whole new culture. But I gained something I never would have had in my country of origin. I gained a life that has been extremely rewarding and allowed me to develop so I could positively impact the lives of others."*

*The adversity of being abruptly uprooted and adjusting to a new country brought out the strengths in Antonio. His tenacity, courage, vision and commitment helped him turn detours into tour de forces. I honestly believe my husband can do anything he wants to do, and I've watched him achieve things he didn't think were possible.*

The second story is about Ann Barton, a woman I met through my radio program. She is a very faithful listener and calls in often with her inspirational thoughts. It wasn't until I brought Ann in to co-host the show with me several times that I learned about the remarkable strength behind this woman.

*Ann has been married over forty years to the same man and often talks about how she is still attracted to him. She lost her two sons to AIDS and battled breast cancer all within a two-year period. There is no bitterness in her heart. Ann said, "I learned from my mother at a very young age to go forward with my life by accepting those things I can't change and changing the things I can change. We have two choices when we meet life's blows. We can wallow in self-pity for what we've lost or we can go forward with beautiful memories of the things we valued most." About her sons who died she said, "I had two loving sons and I have good memories of them. One of my sons had a beautiful daughter who is his legacy. She is smart and is as beautiful on the inside as she is on the outside. Ann told the story of her discovery of breast cancer.*

*"When my surgeon told me I had cancer, I got a sinking feeling in my stomach but remained outwardly calm and composed. When he asked me if I wanted a second opinion, I said, 'No, let's get on with it.' When he asked me when I wanted to have the surgery, I said, 'Yesterday.' Within less than a week I had a biopsy, a lumpectomy, and then ultimately a mastectomy. After the surgery, I began exercising and stretching the shoulder. Within two weeks, I was on horseback."*

As a result of her experience, Ann wrote an inspiring poem. The last verse is particularly powerful:

*I must weather the storms on the rolling seas,*
*Meet the challenges God gave to me;*
*Take His hand when He reaches out;*
*Put my trust in Him, His love receive;*
*Pray the prayers my mother taught;*
*And have the courage to believe.*

On the philosophy that makes her who she is, Ann said, "I have learned to eliminate the negative. There's as old song whose lyrics are 'accentuate the positive, eliminate the negative' and that's just what I try to do. God gave us stumbling blocks and mountains to climb in order to make us stronger. We need to think of what we have instead of what we don't have. I learned from my father that if we're willing to make sacrifices, we can be whatever we want to be. For some reason, I have always met the challenge, because I wanted to prove myself worthy."

The third story is about a woman whom I've gotten to know through working with her on projects at our local hospital, and was a guest on Positive Living with her husband Chris.

Linda Larko married a man who is a quadriplegic. She met him after his accident, which left him with no movement from his shoulders down. I will never forget Linda saying to me, "I was married before to a man who had the use of his arms and legs, and he was more handicapped than Chris. He was not a creative thinker and so often didn't know what to do, so he just wouldn't do anything. There was no joyfulness in him. Chris is fully alive and will try all kinds of things, including racing with his wheel chair. He's a creative thinker and has helped me grow to be a creative

82

*thinker. Even though he can't move his arms and legs like other people, he moves his head a certain way that communicates his confidence and assertiveness. Chris is very strong in character. Although we're both independent people, we're very open to each other's needs."*

*I asked Chris how he has changed since the accident. "I've lost a lot of extra baggage such as pride," he said, "and I've gained things like patience and humility. It takes more than just what one human being can do on his own. It takes God and I know that He's with me no matter what the circumstances are. I know that He's got the strength and He'll see me through."*

*I asked Chris how Linda has helped him turn his detour into a triumph. "It's something we do everyday," he chorused. "Morning, noon and night, we thank God for our blessings."*

I felt honored to meet this young couple and to share their story. The genuiness and sincerity in their voices confirmed their oneness and happiness. His accident brought them together. What had been a major detour in his life had produced an enduring relationship. Chris recently died, but his amazing spirit lives on. I will always remember the sparkle in his eyes and the affection he had for Linda.

Stories like these teach us how others gathered their strength to overcome difficult experiences. When people "hit bottom" and then work through their problems, they are much stronger and often reach greater heights than they would have before. When we listen, there is a voice within us that calls to us and offers us a road map. But it takes belief, vision, time, patience, trust and dedication.

The following story, which illustrates this beautifully, is about an extraordinary woman who came to appreciate her own self-worth. Jackie Waldman, author of *The Courage to Give: Inspiring Stories of People Who Triumphed Over Tragedy to Make a Difference in the World.* was chosen by CNN as one of their millennium heroes. She tells stories of national heroes who have gone beyond their pain to help other and contribute to a better world.

Her book grew out of her own heroic story, which she shared on Positive Living:

> *In 1991 when I was diagnosed with multiple sclerosis, I was devastated. I was sad, angry and scared. I spent the next few years trying every treatment possible to find a cure that does not exist. My husband and three children were happy*
>
> *I was alive, but I couldn't understand why they didn't feel my pain. I was a poster child for self-pity.*
>
> *It was not until I saw Steven Spielberg's movie, "Schindler's List" that this all turned around for me. I realized that real survival isn't about a disease. It depends on how we treat each other. I became really grateful for my own life for the first time since I had been diagnosed. Thankfully, I developed a new perspective and a new purpose. My gratitude prompted me to write this book.*

Through her own personal tragedy, Jackie Waldman found the courage to move beyond her own pain and disbelief. She could have given up. She could have used her illness as an excuse to lash out at the world and retreat into a life of self-imposed exile. Fortunately, she accepted her illness and became grateful for what she could do and for the contributions she could make by helping others move beyond their limitations. Lewis Mumford pays tribute to people like Jackie when he says, "There is a kind of release that comes directly to those who have undergone an ordeal and know, having survived it, that they are equal to life's challenges."

I am reminded of what psychologist, Victor Frankl said when he described the fate of those who lived in the concentration camps. "We, who lived in concentration camps, can remember those who walked through the huts comforting others, giving away their last piece of bread. They may have been few in number, but they offer sufficient proof that everything can be taken from a person but one thing: the last of human freedoms – to choose one's attitude in any given set of circumstances – to choose one's own way."

## *Checkmate Your Ego*

*Ego boundaries must be hardened before they can be softened. Identity must be established before it can be transcended. One must find one's self before one can lose it. Our limits are our ego's limits. When we extend our limits through love, we move beyond the ego.*

(M. Scott Peck, MD)

*T*here is a famous story about a learned university professor who was well known and respected world wide for his work in alternative medicine.

*The professor decided to visit a wise old doctor with a similar specialty, who lived across town. The professor was writing a book and wanted to ask his old mentor a few questions and discuss several curiosities.*

*The old man received the self-assured professor in his library, and an attendant served tea. As soon as the professor seated himself, he began boasting about his academic success, his considerable medical credentials and his expertise in their shared field. The old doctor said nothing as he poured tea into his boastful guest's cup. The professor hardly noticed the old doctor's hospitality and kept talking about his own accomplishments.*

*Suddenly the professor realized that his host was still pouring tea into an already overflowing cup. The hot tea was spilling over the table and onto the hardwood floor.*

*"Stop," cried the professor. "What are you doing? You're spilling all of the tea."*

*The old doctor looked at his puzzled colleague and smiled softly.*

*"Just as the cup cannot hold anymore tea once it's filled," he replied, "how can I give you the information you need when your ego is so full?"*

As the old doctor demonstrated so dramatically, we cannot listen to anyone else's advice or wise counsel if we are full of ourselves. The young professor in this story seemed to be "full of himself." He was egotistical and egocentric. He probably never talked about anyone else because he always talked about himself. He certainly was not ecumenical in praising others or listening to their advice.

Someone once told me that *ego* means "easing God out." I think that applies to people who can't keep their ego in check. All of us have egos and most people have healthy egos. A healthy ego contributes to a high level of self-esteem and confidence in oneself. Every one of us exists in a constantly changing world, which places our individuality at the center. We are all at the core of our own world and our ego is the conscious connection between our self-concept and the other *selves* around us. The psychiatrist, Karen Horney, contends that "our energies are directed toward realizing our own potentialities." With the help of our ego we sometimes create and protect a false, idealized self, which is based on pride and self-preservation.

In the story I shared earlier, the young professor wanted the advice and counsel of the old doctor, but felt threatened at the same time. He used his egocentrism and pride as defense mechanisms to protect his fragile ego. My father shares a story of a biblical character who did not let his prideful ego get in the way and the outcome was a much happier one than our young professor experienced:

*This is the story of the Israelites in the desert. Moses is acting as judge and jury over the multitude of problems and disputes of the day. Actually, he was a one-man judicial system and was burdened with the load. Jethro, who was Moses father-in-law and a Midianite, not an Israelite, comes to visit him and sees what Moses is going through.*

*Jethro asks, "Why are you doing this all by yourself? Why don't your organize other worthy people to be judges? You can have them handle the cases in groups of tens, twenties or fifties and thereby you will decentralize what you are doing."*

*Moses learns from his father-in-law how to serve the people better and he instituted a system of jurisprudence that was the forerunner of our judicial system. It relieved Moses of the burden*

> *and gave the people greater access to decision-makers who could help them with their problems. So here is Jethro, an outside source who comes in on the scene, looks at that's going on and immediately spots the problem. Moses recognized that Jethro's advice made sense and adopted it. Many of us receive the right advice, but reject it out of hand. Moses didn't let his ego get in the way of accepting sound advice.*

Moses held his ego in check. He was careful not to let pride get in his way. He recognized that our ego influences our behavior more than any other single factor in our make-up. It is our chief perceptual filter. We perceive the world – its events, objects and people – through the ego's view of the world. Great leaders like Moses use their common sense, extraordinary judgment and critical thinking to checkmate their egos. Abraham Maslow would call Moses a self-actualized individual. Wayne Dyer would refer to him as a "no limit" person. According to Swiss psychologist, Carl Jung, Moses would be a "transcendent self," capable of controlling the ego and moving toward an individuated human being.

My father's story about Moses and Jethro shows that Moses was able to put his own ego aside and listen to good advice. It is a great lesson for all of us.

# *Analyze Your Anger*

> *People who fly into a rage usually make a*
> *bad landing.*    (Will Rogers)

*I*sn't it interesting that anger is just one letter short of *danger*? Anger is dangerous emotional territory with a capital "D." It has the power to devastate relationships, ruin the earth and destroy people. Anger is a defense mechanism. People tend to get angry when they feel threatened or pressured. Anger begins as an inner feeling of unrest and agitation. We sense it and try to control it long before it explodes into an emotional grenade. The problem with anger is that, unharnessed, it tends to wreck logical, rational, life-supporting decisions.

On the positive side, anger can also be a productive emotion. Feeling anger lets us know that we're alive and vital. Anger serves as a motivator, because it propels us to take action. Anger has been the catalyst to create organizations and foundations, champion causes, and honor memorials.

On my radio program, C. C. Nuckols, co-author of *Healing an Angry Heart: Finding Solace in a Hostile World*, discussed how to find a safe place for ourselves by harnessing our anger into positive energy. He said, "Some people hold it in, which is very destructive to the cardiovascular system. Some people let it out by putting down other people, being critical or sometimes hurting themselves by taking drugs and other things to mask it. On the positive side, some people use their anger as constructive energy. I found that a lot of folks who successfully deal with anger have been able to use it as an energy source. They derived benefit from it by using it as a motivational call to action."

I asked Dr. Nuckols how we can use anger constructively. He said, "You can use anger as positive energy by walking away for a few minutes to construct an action plan that allows you to gain some level of control. This is in tune with good communication skills and good problem solving skills." He gave specific examples of what to say, "What you said to me made me really angry and this is why..." or, "I am not quite sure where you are coming from and I need to talk to you about it," or "tell me exactly what you mean by this." Is there something that you are being critical of me about that I can improve?"

Dr. Nuckols discussed three categories of coping techniques to deal with anger. He said, "The first heading is relaxation therapy which includes deep breathing and the use of muscle-relaxation training, using images, counting backwards from ten, using hypnotic tapes and changing the tone and tempo of your voice to help calm yourself down. The second major category is behavioral and includes taking time outs, walking away from corrosive situations, and anything you know that will break a pattern."

A coping technique I suggest is to take a breath long enough to pause, because this pause shifts your energy so you can think before you act. Then excuse yourself, walk away and get a breath of fresh air. Feel the anger. Tell the trees, sky, and grass how you feel until the anger is out of your body. Then when you go back into the room, you can deal with the issue at hand.

The third category Dr. Nuckols discussed is cognitive. He said. "This is where we understand that what makes us angry are the things we say to ourselves. Self-taught patterns is another term for it. When we have self-taught patterns that cause us to get angry and to behave poorly, then we should identify those thought-patterns and change them. Most therapy for anger management tends to work with one or all three of those particular types of styles."

Here's my cognitive strategy. When I get angry, I know "my buttons have been pushed" and I find a safe place where, or person with whom, I can vent my feelings. Then, after I've released the intense feelings, I retrace my steps like a detective, to analyze not only the specific issue that triggered the anger, but what, on a deeper level, caused it. Then I let it go and let the healing take it's course. Within a day or two, I either have resolved it in my mind, or I go back to resolve the situation more objectively.

For example, if someone hurts my feelings and I feel diminished, I know it goes back to my childhood when kids made fun of me in school. This is a very sensitive area for me and understanding where it originated does two things. It helps me draw on my understanding of the source when I feel diminished, so I can handle the situation differently. Secondly, it helps me avert situations where I feel I will be diminished.

Dr. C.C. Nuckols and Bill Chickering so poignantly close their book, *Healing an Angry Heart: Finding Solace in a Hostile World,* by saying, "We hope you've learned that although anger can be brutal, it can also be wise. Anger can maim, and anger can heal. Anger can be unfair, and it can be just. Anger can spur us to action, or it can stop us dead in our tracks. Anger can lift our self-esteem, or it can move us to self-pity or remorse. Anger can show us what is wrong with us and with our world, and it can alert us to what wrongs need to be set straight. Anger can be fair, and it can take sides. Anger can bring us to tears and it can bring us to joy. Anger can make us lash out, or it can help us hold back."

Gandhi learned this secret and asserted, "I have learnt through bitter experience the one supreme lesson to conserve my anger, and as heat conserved is transmuted into energy, even so our anger controlled can be transmuted into a power which can move the world."

*Move Through Your Fears*

*Fear imprisons, faith liberates; fear paralyzes, faith empowers; fear disheartens, faith encourages; fear sickens, faith heals; fear makes useless, faith makes serviceable.*
(Harry Emerson Fosdick)

ear is the greatest obstacle we face, because it stops us cold. We have all faced fear about loss – whether it is loss of friends, family, respect, jobs, self-worth, money or possessions. It is when we reach out of our comfort zone, look our fears squarely in the eye, admit them, shiver, and then take the step anyway, that we can succeed. My greatest fear has always been rejection and ridicule. Yet, I've chosen a visible path through my work in the media. My desire to get the message out is greater than my fear, so I've been able to lick the wounds, heal the bumps and bruises, and get on the path again. When my fear reoccurs, it's easier to deal with and I have more confidence because I've been there before and I've gotten through it. I believe in the saying "God doesn't give us any more than we can handle." But God doesn't force us to handle it either. That's up to us.

Anger and fear are related. Holding these emotions inside can be like an explosion waiting to happen somewhere in your body and anywhere during your day. We have

92

discussed how anger can be channeled and controlled. It can be catalyst or catastrophe. Fear, on the other hand, can immobilize us. It can stop us in our tracks. For some people, fear is like being up against a wall, an invisible barrier that keeps them from moving forward. They are unable to move because they are afraid to move.

Fear is something to be moved through, not something to turn from. Dr. Donald Dossey, a guest on my show who helps people overcome phobias is the author of *Keying: The Power of Positive Feelings*. He says that if you can see beyond fear to the goal, you can surround yourself with people that help you move through the fear.

Some fears are normal. For example, if friends want you to learn to ski by starting you on the high slopes, your fear of skiing out-of-control, going too fast or crashing into trees along the slope may be well founded. Fear, in this case, may be a warning signal that says there is a better, safer way for a novice to learn.

There is another aspect of working through fear. It is simply having "blind faith." Blind faith comes into play when we run into dead ends and reach out blindly because there is no light. When we resort to blind faith, we must bridle our fears. My father relates that "One of the most poignant moments in the Bible is when the children of Israel are told by God that, 'If you will hearken to My voice and keep My covenant, you will be My people.' They respond with the words, 'We will do.' The rabbis point out that the children of Israel obeyed without even knowing what was expected of them. They didn't say, 'We'll listen first and then we will decide.'"

My father uses this as an example of blind faith. He emphasizes that "since we don't know how long the trip is, Judaism says to repent one day before you die. Since you don't know when that is, you should repent every day." To me, my father is saying that we should live every day to the fullest – without letting our fears get in the way.

A great historical example of not letting fear stop you involves one of our great presidents in March of 1933. Banks were closing, factories were idle, hundreds of thousands of people were unemployed, an economic depression was crippling the nation, fear was running rampant. Millions of Americans waited expectantly beside their radios, wondering what the new president was going to say.

Franklin Delano Roosevelt knew he was facing an unprecedented crisis in our nation's history. He knew the paralyzing effects of fear, how it could demoralize people and how it could ruin a nation. He steadied himself and spoke boldly, giving one of the most dramatic and compelling speeches in American history:

*This great nation will endure as it has endured, will revive and will prosper. So first of all, let me assert my firm belief that the only thing we have to fear is fear itself – nameless, unreasoning, unjustified terror which paralyzes needed efforts to convert retreat into advance..."*

"The only thing we have to fear is fear itself." These unforgettable words from our president ring true and gave millions of Americans hope and courage. An entire nation trusted Franklin D. Roosevelt and followed him in blind faith through one of the darkest chapters in our history. Fear could have robbed our country of its destiny, and it can rob us of our future if we allow fear to take over. Someone once told me that fear is an acronym. It stands for "false evidence appearing real." The reality is we can move beyond our fears through positive thinking, positive actions and positive living.

# *Use Your Experiences as Lessons to Rewrite Endings*

*As human beings, our greatness lies not so much in being able to remake the world...as in being able to remake ourselves.*
(Mahatma Gandhi)

*O*ne of the rewards of working through our fears is that when we make mistakes, they become our greatest teachers. Years ago, I was at a business holiday party, and met a man who set up roundtable meetings for CEO's of Fortune 500 companies. I asked him if those top executives had anything in common. He said, "Yes, they're not afraid to make mistakes. They use their mistakes to learn, and to propel them to make the next decision."

From our earliest childhood memories of falling down when we initially learned to walk, we learned that making mistakes is part of the process of growth. This lesson gets harder to accept when mistakes cost us friendships, income, work and health. Once we have learned those lessons, we can use past mistakes to help us figure out what to do next. Good second marriages and jobs are examples of this "second chance" learning. The proof of the pudding is when you take ingredients from your past experiences to create a new recipe that helps rewrite the ending.

My first marriage was to a good man of my faith from a prominent family, and I focused on what would be the right thing to do, not on my inner needs. Twelve years after my divorce, I married again, but this time I paid attention to my personal needs and married a man with whom I share the same values and thinking. The relationship with my first husband just wasn't right for me, yet we are good friends to this day. I am thankful for the experience because it taught me a whole new way of thinking. But even more than that, that marriage brought forth into the world my beautiful daughter, Laura. In the final analysis for me, there was no mistake, only a lesson.

I recall my father telling me that there are three Hebrew words which are pillars in Judaism: faith, repentance, and charity. I translate them in the following way. I always had faith that I would someday find the right person. The repentance was the time I spent analyzing my mistakes and working through them. The charity is the years I have spent helping other people find the right role models through my apprenticeship in the media. My Positive Living show is an outgrowth of that involvement and this book is an extension of my *beehive* ministry.

I have found that when you are living in a time of diminished returns, negative circumstances and personal downturns, your attitude and behavior will feel the effects of the pressure. You move cautiously through each day and feel emotionally paralyzed, which keeps you closed. Once you believe you are living in a time of regeneration, your activities tend to be more positive and open. You expect good things to happen. Research has shown for quite some time that we get what we expect to get. People who are able to take change in stride and "roll with the punches" tend to rewrite endings to match their positive expectations. They view the changes they know they must make as opportunities, and not threats. Their attitudinal lenses are colored with positive, growth-oriented thoughts and feelings.

Without sacrificing realism, I encourage you to experiment with the changes you know you must make to live a more balanced, enriched and joyful life. What you do today, both internally and externally, determines how that future will look. "People are always blaming their circumstances for what they are," says George Bernard Shaw. "The people who get on in this world are the people who get up and look for the circumstances they want and if they can't find them, make them."

Whatever the impetus is behind your own pathfinding expedition, you must realize that the only stability you will find is the foot you are standing on. Each step you take involves a suspended foot. If you identify your progress with the suspended foot – you may panic, believing you aren't on solid ground. Your stability lies in your progress. Each step you take rewrites the ending. You may wander off the path occasionally. You may even stumble when you are on the *right* path. That's the nature of pathfinding. My friend and professional coach Bobbi Gemma, who is quoted several times in this book, sent me a card recently with a beautiful picture of a path, explaining how difficult it is to see our own path because we are standing on it.

The steps we take are based on the choices we make, and the choices we make are based on the values, beliefs and experiences that have defined us all of our lives. We are the products of what Joel and Michelle Levey, co-authors of *Living In Balance*, refer to as, "what is developing and dissolving, what is manifesting and potentializing… movement and flexibility…stuckness and resistance to change."

When we wander from our path – as we certainly will occasionally – we need to ask ourselves questions like: What cues did we overlook or misinterpret? What assumptions, expectations and attitudes derailed us? What lessons can we learn now that will keep us squarely on the path? How can we use a particular experience to rewrite the ending to the next similar experience? How can we use our imperfections to perfect our lives?

My father says, "If you have faith and belief, you can create pluses somewhere down the line. Hardships teach us something we may not be aware of at the time. Life teaches us to work harder, to look at things differently, and to organize our lives in a positive direction so we can write our own next chapter. We are the authors of what happens to us."

## *Positive Pollination*

### List:
❖ An old attitude you replaced with a new one.
❖ One of your strengths that has compensated a weakness.
❖ What you did to "rewrite the ending" of a "mistake" you made.
❖ A challenge you have overcome because your inner strength guided you.

### Reflect on:
❖ Old attitudes, beliefs and behaviors that are no longer part of your value system.
❖ Important personal and professional endings you've rewritten.
❖ How you turned a crisis into an opportunity.
❖ How putting your ego aside helped you to see more clearly.
❖ How you worked through your anger in a positive way.
❖ How you worked through a fearful situation in a positive way.

CHAPTER FOUR

# Honor Your Innate Gifts, Talents and Abilities

*Use what talents and abilities you possess. The woods would be very silent if no birds sang there except those that sang best.*

(Henry Van Dyke)

*E*veryone has talent. I have never met a person who does not have some kind of talent, even if it wasn't apparent to them. Some people are certainly more gifted than others in certain areas. One person's talent may lie in singing, while another individual is an amazing sculptor. Other people are talented in the area of medicine, mathematics, chemistry or science. Some people can out-jump, out-run, out-climb and out-smart others.

All of us have special gifts, but some of us discount them or take them for granted for any number of reasons. Others, like Erma Bombeck, appreciate their talents and use them. "When I stand before God at the end of my life," she says, "I hope I won't have a single bit of talent left and will say, 'God, I used everything you gave me.'"

Joan Mills said something very similar. She said, "I'd gone through my life believing in the strength and competence of others; never in my own. Now, dazzled, I've discovered that my capacities are real. It is like finding a fortune in the lining of an old coat."

One way you can discover your innate abilities is to listen to what people say about you, how they compliment you. For example, suppose someone says to you, "Oh, you are such a great writer" or "I really value you as a friend," or, "You work so well with people, you must be a people person." Pay attention to what people tell you, especially when they compliment you.

I have found in my own life that it is important to recognize, accept, use and build on my talents. People tell me I am a strong networker, catalyst, motivator and interviewer. When I question myself or wonder how effective I have been, I think of the inspiring words of Dr. Martin Luther King, Jr.: "If a person sweeps streets for a living, he should sweep them as Michelangelo painted, as Beethoven composed, as Shakespeare wrote."

I believe we are talented because we work at it. Dan Millman said in his book, *No Ordinary Moments*, that "natural talent is overrated...The successful professionals I know in the fields of athletics, acting, law, medicine and business attribute their success more to hard work than to natural talent."

I believe that raw talent coupled with hard work is an unstoppable combination. I also believe that when you consistently honor your innate gifts, talents and abilities you will meet with success beyond your wildest dreams.

# *Be True to Your Life's Purpose*

*Within each of us...there is a gnawing hunger*
*for fulfillment, an undeniable demand for joy,*
*an inestimable sense of purpose, for knowing*
*who we are.*                                    (Eknath Easwaran)

*T*his striving for individuality and transformation is
what Meister Eckhart calls the "pauper becoming
the prince." I believe he is right. The search for our purpose
in life takes us from pauper to prince or princess. It is our
journey toward individuation, as Carl Jung, the Swiss psychologist, calls it; self-actualization according to Abraham
Maslow; and, as Jean Houston says, becoming a possible
human. For many people, finding their purpose becomes a
life-long search. Others seem to find it early on in their
quest for selfhood. But this "gnawing hunger for fulfillment" is very much part of us and is to be found in the same
place, no matter who we are or where we go to find it.

The place where our special purpose resides is illustrated in the following story.

*A small precocious bear cub was inquisitive and*
*daring, completely awestruck with the world around*
*her. She spent hours watching bees fly in and out of*
*the hive and she was fascinated by their persistence,*
*commitment and loyalty to the queen.*

*One day the cub asked her father bear, "Father, I*
*smell a haunting fragrance. It smells so special, so*
*sweet, but I can't quite put my nose on it. What is it?*
*Where is it coming from?"*

*"Why don't you go deeper into the forest with the*
*other animals to see if it comes from any of them?"*
*the father bear suggested.*

103

*So the cub approached a beautiful deer and smelled her rich hide.*

*No, it's not her, the bear cub said to herself.*

*She went up to a fox.*

*"No, it's definitely not him," she said knowingly.*

*She met with the same result in her encounters with an old owl, a pair of rabbits, a school of fish and a chipmunk. She went to all of the animals in the forest. Finally, baffled and a bit tired, the bear cub returned to her den and reported her experiences to her father.*

*"I have gone everywhere, seen everything and listened to everyone," she said sadly, "and none of them has the perfume."*

*The father bear smiled wisely and watched a bee buzz swiftly past them before he spoke.*

*"My lovely young daughter," he spoke softly, "pick up your paw and smell the top of your coat."*

*The cub lifted her paw, gave her thick coat a sniff, and let out a squeal of joy.*

*"It comes from me," she cheered. "The perfume comes from me."*

This is more than just a cute story. It captures the essence of our search for selfhood. The path to our purpose is an inner path. It is the fragrance of our own essence. Our purpose is not something we *discover*, it's something we *uncover*. Finding our purpose answers the question, "Why am I here?"

Two more questions you should ask yourself are, "What path have I chosen?" and "Am I on the right path?" In *Success, Your Dream and You*, I outlined the QPN Model which helps match your personal and professional *qualities* to the needs of your client or friend.

Each letter represents a key component in the QPN Model. **Q** stands for QUALITIES, which are the qualities you bring to the situation such as empathy, competence and efficiency. The **P** stands for PURPOSE, which is your purpose in working with the other person or group. An example of your purpose is to help the other party create win-win situations, where everyone involved is satisfied with the outcomes. The **N** represents the NEEDS of your clients in a business setting or your friends and family in a personal setting. You create a win-win situation when your **P=N**, your purpose is equal to your client's need so that everyone is satisfied with the outcomes. When you also match your qualities, the **Q**, to their needs, the **N**, you and the other party can relate more easily to each other. In this situation to help them create win-win situations, the other party needs the qualities of empathy, competence and efficiency that we outlined above.

Networking is one of my **Q**'s, or qualities. It's a gift I've been given and it comes easily to me. Networking is about building relationships, and investing time and energy in dealing with people to find out what their needs are and how you can match them with yours. I'm describing the QPN model I discussed earlier because I feel it is the backbone of dealing with others and creating win-win relationships. When you create win-win situations as you network and negotiate you will find strife and confusion diminish because you are genuinely working on the other person's behalf while honoring your own needs. Networking takes persistence and negotiation, but it's gentle persuasion that makes you more accessible in the exchange.

Barry Maher, author of *Filling The Glass: The Skeptic's Guide to Positive Thinking in Business* and guest on Positive Living, discussed the importance of being able to relate to your clients or customers. He said, "If you sell yourself out you may find that nobody else is buying. I talk about 'bringing out the prospect in yourself.' And what I mean by that is that you've got to learn to empathize with those you're trying to reach, those you're trying to influence. Whether you selling a product or yourself or your vision or ideas, nobody buys from somebody they can't relate to. That means you have to be 'relatable.' Being 'relatable' is not about selling out or being phony, and it's not about manipulation. It's about understanding the person you're dealing with and bringing out that aspect of yourself that they can best relate to."

Examine the "relatable" you. You can start with honoring your innate gifts, talents and abilities. Where do your talents and skills lie? What is your philosophy of life and work? Do you use initiative, innovativeness and intuitiveness in your work? How strong are your values and beliefs? Do you have the persistence and drive of a pathfinder? When is the last time you asked yourself, "What is my purpose in life?" Do you have a well-defined personal mission statement? Are you any closer now than you were a year ago to expressing your true purpose?

Using these questions based on the QPN Model can help you target your pathfinding. True pathfinding is a growth process. It weaves your skills, talents and abilities into a positive alignment so you can reach your personal and professional vision of success. The QPN Model gives you a carefully constructed framework for measuring your pathfinding progress. For more information on the QPN Model, I invite you to read chapters three and four in *Success, Your Dream and You.*

Once we know our purpose, there's a steadiness, a purposefulness, which seems to guide our actions. According to Mary Wollstonecraft Shelley, "Nothing contributes so much to tranquilize the mind as a steady purpose – a point on which the soul may fix its intellectual eye."

I believe she makes an important distinction between the mind and the soul's intelligence. The more I study life and the more insights I get from the guests on Positive Living, I'm inclined to believe that the purpose of our experiences in the physical world is to prompt us to look at ourselves more closely, to examine the core of our being, to come to the realization that we are the unique expression of our own special purpose.

My father tells this story:

> *A very wealthy man in town approached a poor carpenter who had been struggling all his life. He says, "I'm going away for a year and I want you to build me a house. I am going to give you all the money you need to do it right. I want the best of everything that you can get to build the house. As the carpenter began building the house he says to himself, "The owner isn't going to know the difference. Why should I use all this expensive stuff when I can put in cheap imitations and pocket the difference." So he builds the house as cheaply as he can. The rich man comes back and the carpenter gives him the house key. The rich man says to the carpenter, 'No, here. The key is for you. I wanted to build the house for you, so I am giving you the house as a present.' The moral of the story is be careful, don't cheat because you may be cheating yourself.*

Being true to your own purpose is the ultimate accomplishment in life. In the entertainment industry it would be called the lifetime achievement award. All of us are born with the wherewithal to express our purpose. Honeybees are born with the instinct and ability to make honey. It is their life calling. Nature has provided all of its offsprings with an instinct toward self-fulfillment. All we have to do is to honor our life's purpose.

## *Set Realistic Stretch Goals*

*It is good to have an end to journey toward; but it is the journey that matters in the end.*
(Ursula K. LeGuin)

*I* have used Ursula LeGuin's quote to introduce this brief mention of the importance of goals because she emphasizes the process of achieving our goals. Her insight fits perfectly with the theme of this book which is pathfinding, not path completion. Travelers on the road to success must know where they are going, but they must also concentrate on the present. They must let each day's work absorb their energies, talents and abilities so they can blaze a path toward selfhood. And if they do, as Henry David Thoreau assures us, "If they advance confidently in the direction of their dreams and endeavor to live the life which they have imagined, they will meet with a success unexpected in common hours."

Pathfinding is advancing – sometimes confidently, sometimes painfully – in the direction of our dreams. It is taking positive steps and setting realistic long-term goals. True pathfinding means moving beyond words and translating goals into experience. It means consistency of purpose. One of my favorite stories about consistency of purpose, the ability to focus on meaningful goals without being distracted or misled, involves Mother Teresa. I learned the story from Dr. Louis Tartaglia, psychiatrist, noted author and one of my popular co-hosts. Dr. Tartaglia had the opportunity to meet with Mother Teresa several times.

Dr. Tartaglia is the narrator of the audio program which he co-wrote with Father Angelo Scolozzi, *Thirsting for God: Spiritual Lessons of Mother Teresa.* On my program, Dr. Tartaglia said:

> *"Mother Teresa was a warm and compassionate, spiritual messenger with a single-minded message. She lived to minister to the poorest of the poor. She never deviated from it. Even when she visited the Pope at the Vatican, her attention was focused on the poor. At one point she forgot why she was there." Father Angelo asked how she could possibly forget why she was there. Mother Teresa told him, "I was looking at all of those rooms. Some weren't being used. I was thinking how many beds we could put in there for the poor, and how many of the poor we could take care of."*

Mother Teresa never took her eyes off her goal. Everything she saw and experienced was bound to her personal goals. Her every impulse was goal management and goal attainment. Although her ultimate goal – taking care of the poorest of the poor – was her stretch goal, she saw each day as going down the home stretch toward that goal. She didn't miss an opportunity to move a step closer to her goal.

Mother Teresa's story is similar to other successful people's stories when it comes to goal achievement. Anna Pavlova, the famous Russian ballerina said, "To tend unfailingly, unflinchingly, towards a goal, is the secret of success." Washington Irving, American essayist, believed that "great minds have purposes and others only have wishes." Peter Drucker says that goals "are not fate, they are direction…They are the means to mobilize resources and energies…to make the future." Much like Anna Pavlova, Mother Teresa said, "in just one direction, not every direction."

Dr. Steve Levinson, a guest on Positive Living and co-author of *Following Through: A Revolutionary New Model for Finishing Whatever You Start*, gave this advice for people who are having difficulty sticking to their goal. "You have to arrange your circumstances so that you will follow through. You can't count on your desire for results alone to get those results for them. It won't work. You need more than that. When you're on a diet, for example, you have to think about what's going to move you, what's going to keep you moving. Not just what's going to get you started, but what's going to help you finish. That might mean making promises to other people. It might be hanging around with people in whose company you tend more to do the right thing. You almost have to look at the situation ahead of time in your mind's eye."

The following story illustrates an insightful quote by William Jennings Bryan, "Destiny is not a matter of chance, it is a matter of choice; it is not a thing to be waited for, it is a thing to be achieved."

*Tim McCullen ,at the age of 37, is the president of Window Gang, the largest residential window and pressure cleaning company in America. Tim came from a family business where he began working every day after school at the age of six.*

*He spent the summer after high school graduation at the beach, where he went door-to-door with two squeegees, washing salt spray from windows, sometimes trading services for food. To compensate for his fear of heights, he hired friends to help him. By the end of the summer, he had almost all the accounts at the beach.*

*When his parents decided to sell the family business, Tim realized he could transform his part-time window washing business into a full time venture.*

*The business grew to become the largest residential cleaning company in America. The Window Gang was ranked number 51 among 200 in SUCCESS Magazine's Franchisee Satisfaction for franchisee/ franchiser relations, specifically in the areas of trust and communication, product and passion, leadership, training, support and respect.*

*On Tim's key to success he said, "I've always had a sense of urgency. We always lived like there is no tomorrow. If a crew called me to tell me that they were finished for the day, I'd call the next day's customer, tell them that there was an opening and send the crew there ahead of schedule. We were there when we told customers we'd be there We're always out there fast. We always give an estimate and we always call back. We never stop calling until we hear a yes or a no. That kind of service really helped us to grow our markets."*

*On advice to young people who want to be successful, Tim said, "You have to stay focused and put a goal on paper. It's kind of like a road map. Without one, you don't know where you are going. "I also think that you have to learn responsibility. Nothing was handed to me growing up and it served me well. Parents who give their children things without them working for it do not teach them how to reach their goals."*

*Giving back is also part of Tim's philosophy and success. When a good friend and competitor got prostate cancer and almost lost his business, Tim had the Window Gang do his work for him. After he paid his employees their usual percentage, Tim gave his competitor the rest of the money and did not try to take his clients.*

*What's the greatest meaning behind success for Tim McCullen and The Window Gang? "We created something. I started from scratch, it wasn't a family business and I knew nothing about it. Here I was walking down the streets of Wrightsville Beach as a one-man operation in 1986. Now in 2002, we're the largest residential window and pressure cleaning company in America!*

In your own pathfinding, use your insight as much as your eyesight. Tim realized he had to make his franchise more successful so he could attain his dreams. Goals are inner visions recorded on paper. They are dreams with time limits. Pathfinding is about goal-realization, but it's also about self-realization. When selfhood is the goal, goals become the means instead of the ends. I believe goals are realistic when they stretch you toward becoming what you are meant to become. So reach for the stars along the path, but keep your feet on solid ground by taking one step at a time.

## *Follow the 5 P's to Success*

*You can have anything you want...if you want it badly enough. You can be anything you want to be, do anything you set out to accomplish if you hold to that desire with singleness of purpose.*

(Abraham Lincoln)

*O*nce you match your purpose/vision to your beliefs, you can begin to develop your plan around them to meet your goals in life. When your beliefs are really part of you, they show up in everything you do; the organizations you join, the programs you listen to, the movies you watch, the friends you associate with, and the clients you do business with. Your beliefs don't escape you. When you think they do, they sneak out from wherever you've been hiding them. They're part of you, and you should be proud of them.

In *Success, Your Dream and You*, I outline my 5 P's to success, which I feel complement the seven keys to successful pathfinding. They are purpose, plan, passion, persistence and patience. Your purpose guides you, your plan focuses you, your passion motivates you, your persistence gives you new direction and keeps you going when the going gets tough and your patience brings you the trust and faith to stay on your path.

Finding your purpose has been discussed here at length. The plan is the concrete action derived from your vision. There are so many books written on goal setting and action plans, but the easiest way to develop a plan is to write your wish list, check off those wishes you feel are realistic, number those and break down those wishes into small manageable pieces that you can easily accomplish them. Tasks which are too big are often seen as mountains and cause people to procrastinate. Ralph Waldo Emerson wrote, "The reward of a thing well done is to have done it."

Passion is an instant self-motivator because when you are passionate about what you do, you just do it seemingly without effort. Jonathan Winters says, "If your ship doesn't come in, swim out to it!" But when you don't have passion, you probably won't "swim out to it." When you have passion, you're likely to swim to the ship, no matter where it is.

W. J. Davidson writes, "The life that conquers is the life that moves with a steady resolution and persistence toward a predetermined goal. Those who succeed are those who thoroughly learned the immense importance of plan in life, and the tragic brevity of time." An example of persistence is given by Jill Lawrence, national award-winning journalist and host of "Jill & Friends," who interviews best-selling authors, experts and everyday people in the field of self-help and personal enrichment. On the recurring theme that she hears about success on her radio program, Ms. Lawrence said on Positive Living, "The number one most important trait from a person who wants to achieve success in any arena, appears to be persistence. Time and time and time again I hear someone say that.

"The person that said it the most clearly to me was James Redfield, author of *Celestine Prophecy* which, in the category of hardback books, is the number one best selling book in publishing history. I said to James on my radio program, 'That's extraordinary. How can you even imagine that?' And he replied, 'I'm not as surprised by my success as I am by the fact that I didn't give up. I could so easily have taken that manuscript and saved it for the grandchildren, but I didn't.' He and Sally put the books in their trunk and did the tour of the southeast, giving the book away. James Redfield believes that because they gave the book away, a lot of other people also passed it on to other people. In fact, that's how I got it. A friend sent it to me. So that set up the whole thing. When people hold tight to their last quarter or their pile of gold or whatever, they are holding on and refusing to let it be moved."

Persistence involves more than one person because we all need help to carry our vision and plan. This is where the concept of networking plays a vital role. Our networks help us achieve our goals. Ivan Misner, Ph.D., co-author of New York Times Best-Selling *Masters of Networking* and the founder and CEO of BNI, Business Network International, the largest business networking organization in the world talked about the process behind networking on my Positive Living program. "It's real important for people to understand this process is more about farming than it is about hunting. It's about cultivating relationships with other business professionals. This is not a get rich quick scheme. It's a way to lay the solid foundation for a long-term successful relationship. We don't teach that in the colleges and universities in this country. We teach people how to build multi-million dollar advertising companies and how to close the deal, but we don't teach them how to build relationships. When you ask the average business owner or salesperson what's one of the most important ways to build your business, they'll all say that it is word of mouth."

Of the 5 P's to success, patience is the most challenging for me. Once I see the result in my mind, I want it to happen. Patience doesn't mean just sitting back on the hammock with a drink in your hand and waiting. It means nurturing the seeds you have planted and knowing that some won't grow at all. Some will grow into short stumps, some will grow into bushes and some will grow into tall trees. When you plant the seeds, you don't know which will bear fruit, so you have to plant them all with the same tender loving care. Michelangelo said, "Genius is eternal patience."

Over the past few years, I added a sixth P to my success list – prayer. The power of prayer is an underlying theme in many of the stories and examples in this book, and has been a powerful force in my life. As Mahatma Gandhi said so eloquently, "Prayer is the key of the morning and the bolt of the evening."

## *Use Your Talents Effectively*

*Too many people overvalue what they are not and undervalue what they are.* (Malcolm Forbes)

*K*nowing yourself well enough to tap into your skills is a vital part of pathfinding because because you must know what you love and what your strengths and weaknesses are in order to be truly happy on your path. Dr. Phil McGraw, best-selling author of *Self Matters: Creating Your Life From The Inside Out,* asks readers to list the ten most defining moments of their lives, the seven most critical choices they have made which have put them on their current path and the five most pivotal people in their world who have shaped them. These are key questions to get to the heart of who you are.

A shining example of this is from the award-winning radio program, Plastic Surgery Today, hosted by my husband Dr. Antonio Carbonell. He interviewed Dr. William Magee, plastic surgeon and co-founder of "Operation

116

Smile," a worldwide worldwide organization that repairs congenital cleft-lip and palates in children, who discussed how "Operation Smile" began and grew.

*"Operation Smile was then and still is today about a child. I will never forget there was a little lady aged well beyond her chronological age, I'm sure, that approached me with her daughter at her side. Her daughter had a big hole in her lip from a cleft lip and with tears literally pouring down the mother's cheeks, she gave me a ripe basket of bananas to thank me for trying to take care of her child even though we had turned her away. With tears ultimately coming down my cheeks I knew that we had to do something to go back and help more people. If you and I were to spin a roulette wheel, what would be the chances we would be born who we are and where we are? What would be the chances we would be born in a rice paddy planting rice and plowing fields? The overwhelming odds are that we would be in that rice paddy.*

*"So we have to ask ourselves the question: 'Why was I given this privilege to be who I am and where I am?' The only answer that you can legitimately come up with is: 'To use the talents we have to serve other people.' The beauty is that when you do that you don't lose your success," Dr. Magee continued. "You don't lose your ability to succeed in your individual life. You only augment it.*

*"Operation Smile just evolved from there. We told our friends. They told their friends. And today, twenty years later, we have five thousand medical volunteers on our database. We go to twenty countries, we have taken care of over sixty thousand children for free, all with volunteers. It's not the work that my wife and I did alone. It was us saying to people: 'Let us expose*

*you to what we have been exposed to, and then, if you find it as touching as we have found it to be, then come back and help us.'"*

The work of Dr. Magee and his wife Kathy in co-founding Operation Smile is summed up by Cynthia Kersey, guest on my radio program, Positive Living, who is the author of *UNSTOPPABLE: 45 Powerful Stories of Perseverance and Triumph from People Just Like You.* Cynthia said unstoppable people are ignited by purpose, passion, belief, preparation, team, creativity and persever-ance. She said, "These people stubbornly refuse to quit and ultimately have a good chance of making things happen just because they persevere."

Dr. Magee and his wife started a team made up of fam-ily members. His children started Happy Clubs in high schools, worked with summer youth programs across the country to talk about humanitarian efforts and leadership, and took high school students abroad with Operation Smile. As professional adults, the Magee's children are still involved with starting chapters where they live, fund-raising activities and promotion. This initial family team has grown into a worldwide team. Cynthia Kersey continues, "It really is the extent to which you have the tenacity and resilience to make your dream a reality."

Knowing yourself well enough to use your talents only works when you believe in yourself and your principles. Like the Magees, when you take a stand on your position, you must be willing to stand up for it anywhere, and at any-time. Abraham Lincoln said it well. "I desire so to conduct the affairs of this administration that if at the end I have lost every other friend on earth, I shall at least have one friend left, and that friend shall be down inside of me."

Barry Maher, author of *Filling The Glass: The Skeptic's Guide to Positive Thinking in Business* and guest on Positive

Living, talked about the strategy he calls "Being your own Guru." Barry said, "With all the money we spend on self improvement in this country, you think we'd be darn close to perfect by now. We make guru after guru wealthy for telling us things that for the most part we all believe to be true, then we don't do much of anything about making those things part of our lives. You've got to be your own guru, your own motivator. You've got to start thinking of it as part of your job description. Besides, Tony Robbins can't be around every moment of the day when all those thousands of little decisions that lead toward or away from your goal have to be made."

But you are around yourself every day. You can be your own guru if you conscientiously do the things you know you should do to improve yourself and use your talents effectively. Refuse to undervalue yourself. Value your uniqueness. Fine tune your talents and abilities.

## *Align Money and Values*

*To fulfill a dream, to be allowed to tolerate lonely labor, to be given a chance to create, is the meat and potatoes of life. The money is the gravy.* (Bette Davis)

Some people are financially successful and unhappy. Others are both happy and successful. I believe financial success can equal happiness when money is aligned with values. Money is really neutral in and of itself. It's special printed paper and coin. The value of money is revealed in the values it preserves. If your goal is security, safety, comfort and/or family closeness and you use money to obtain the things that bring you those values, you will most likely be satisfied.

I have always admired people who are prosperous both spiritually and financially because I feel that financial success combined with spiritual success is challenging to achieve. An example of this is the Hamad family, who live in our community. They came to this country about thirty years ago from Palestine. John Hamad built a very successful real estate business from scratch. They are not only one of the most successful families in our community, they are also well respected.

John and his wife Susie have four children all of whom were part of the family business from a very young age. They are all college graduates and very successful entrepreneurs. What is so remarkable about this man and his family is their closeness, the love they give to each other and the stories he always tells with a twinkle in his eye. Although some of the adult children and grandchildren live in the family home, they take care of each other without controlling each other.

John's motto is "love with mercy, act justly, and walk humbly" and he sets this example daily in his life where you can find him happily talking to people from all walks of life. One of our local restaurant owners and his wife said to me, "John really lights up the room. I feel good just being around him." I agree with her and love being with John because of the dynamic energy and joy I feel in his presence. He and his wife Susie have truly combined spirituality with external success and they and their children have blossomed here because of who they are.

Positive people, like John, have their own special language. They speak in positives. They talk about how things are now, how they have worked out. They view problems as part of the process but never lose sight of the positive direction they are going. No matter how bad the situation, they feel hope and believe in forward movement.

One night I was in the ice cream parlor that his son Samer owns and watched as he taught his young son how to scoop the ice cream and put caps on the cups. I marveled over how he was teaching his son the same way his father taught him the business when he was young. John set an example for all of his children who have followed his lead. What impressed me most was the patience Samer had with his son. I was reminded of Winston Churchill's motto, similar to John Hamad's philosophy, which sums up the true values in life. "All the great things are simple, and many can be expressed in single words: freedom; justice; honor; duty; mercy; hope."

On Positive Living, I interviewed Chris Prentiss, author of *The Little Book of Secrets: 81 Secrets for Living A Happy, Prosperous, and Successful Life.* He applies to modern day life one of the world's oldest writings, *The I Ching,* the ancient Chinese "Book of Changes." It consists of 64 symbolic hexagrams that indicate wise courses of action. Success and good fortune are not accidents according to Mr. Prentiss. He said, "These truths are guidelines for action. Being wonderfully happy, having great abundance, experiencing exciting good fortune and being spectacularly successful are not accidents, but the direct result of our actions. We produce results by what we do at every moment. There's an old saying, 'The more you do of what you have done, the more you will get of what you already have.' If you take correct actions to bring about success, happiness and prosperity, you will bring them about as a result of natural law."

Quality versus quantity and having less but enjoying it more, are concepts I've explored on my radio program. Tracey McBride author of *Frugal Luxuries by the Season* and frequent guest on Positive Living, said, "That is a very French philosophy. My friend from France doesn't have a lot of things. She has several wonderful and expensive display pieces in her house, and that's it. It's about recognizing the difference between quality and quantity." She added, "Having less isn't just about spending. It's also about clutter. Clutter stops energy which you need in your life."

She defined the concept of simplicity, "My whole theme for every season is what simplicity is. Minimize the things that won't take you to your goal. We all want happiness. Know what you want and how to get there. We often get sidetracked along the way. Simplicity is learning how not to get side tracked. Once you do that, you are no longer riding on the wave of circumstances and life experiences. "The bottom line," says Tracey, "is cultivate what is truly of value. Things that really matter are time with our loved ones, our inner sense of prosperity and those intangibles that no one can ever take from you."

Another guest, Linda Breen Pierce, author of *Choosing Simplicity: Real People Finding Peace and Fulfillment in a Complex World*, surveyed 211 people of all ages and many cultural backgrounds from 40 states. On my radio program, Linda discussed what simple living really means. She said, "Many people have a myth about simple living. They feel that it involves giving up all the things that they like, when in fact it's a process of figuring out how much is enough. It's not about giving up the things that you really appreciate. It's about giving up the things that you have acquired more out of habit or because you are trying to keep up with others. It's a process of figuring out what things in your life are important."

She advises people who feel stuck in their lifestyles to realize that simplicity is primarily an inside job. The first step is "finding out who you are inside because that is the only way you are going to know what is going to make you happy on the outside." Part of that "finding out" has to do with the realization of what you do well, what you aren't so good at, what your should do and what you should not do.

Again it comes back to values. When you know yourself and your values are clear you will make wise choices. Stephen Bolt, executive director of Values Financial Network and author of *Money for Life* said on my radio program that many people start out backwards, thinking of the money first. He said, "They look at how much money they have and then eliminate what they can't do. They settle for what they have to do to make money. In doing so, they give up their plan, their purpose and ultimately their life."

Stephen talked about the importance of personal integrity. He said, "Make sure you have a solid value system because that is ultimately what is going to govern your life and all the decisions you make in your life. Secondly, make sure that you align everything about your life according to your values and most specifically your money."

In summary Stephen said, "Make a conscious choice about your life, then your purpose and then develop a plan. Next figure out how much money you are going to need, for how long you are going to need it, what increments you are going to need it and how you are going to get it. Then the money is not running your life. Your purpose is running your life and the money becomes the vehicle."

There comes a time when you may have to pay more than usual for what you really value. Barry Maher, whom I quoted earlier in this chapter explained his "Change the Scale" strategy on Positive Living. "Thirty thousand dollars is a lot of money for a Honda," he said, "but for a Rolls Royce it's dirt cheap. It's not how big it is, it's how big it seems. And in exactly the same way, we can change the scale to put our problems into perspective."

This biblical story told and adapted by my father illustrates this point.

*Abraham comes to the land of the Hittites to bury his wife Sarah in a place called Machpeleh. He asked the tribal chieftain for the price of the burial site. The chieftain quotes him a highly inflated price of 400 shekels. Abraham's response is 'What is 400 shekels between you and me? Go, bury your dead.' Abraham pays the money because his goal is to return his wife to her area of birth and fulfill her dying wish.*

*There are two morals to this story. The first is that money is the medium by which you have people do things for you. It allows you to possess items to achieve your goals. The value of money can not be discounted. Obviously the more you have, the easier it is to accomplish these goals. The second moral of the story is to achieve your goals, you may have to put yourself in debt, but don't get in the habit of putting yourself in debt unnecessarily. For example, don't let the ease of use of your credit card divert you from your goal by spending on unnecessary items.*

My father has a saying, "For money you can have honey." For me that means when you have a clear goal, know what you want and have the patience, faith and trust to wait until you are ready financially, you'll be able to have what you want with ease. That always comforts me when I want an item now but need to wait. I know that it will be there. It may be in a different form from what I wanted and may not have the exact features, but it will be there.

Another source of wealth is tithing, which includes tithing your time, talents and money. Thomas Carlyle writes, "The work an unknown good man has done is like a vein of water flowing hidden underground, secretly making the ground green." My father states, "Contributions share the wealth. No society can long exist if everybody is looking to take and nobody is willing to give. The natural tendency is to solicit from well-healed people. When you don't have money, you give of yourself, if you are a giver. If we could get the return on our investments comparable to the return we get of kindness, we would be very wealthy indeed."

# *Be Prepared to Change and Grow*

*Be the change that you want to see in the world.*
(Gandhi)

*R*ichard Bolles, author of *Job Hunting on the Internet, How To find Your Mission in Life,* and *What Color Is Your Parachute?* (the most popular career-planning and job hunting book in the world) discussed on my radio program how your mission in life changes. He said, "I don't think people should try to say, 'My mission in life is and always will be this.' Rather, we need to say, 'This is my mission at this moment.' That is why I wrote *How to Find Your Mission in Life,* which is also in the appendix in the back of *What Color Is Your Parachute,* to reinforce that for people. I use a metaphor of being in a foggy valley and some stranger comes along and says 'Take my hand and I'll guide you if you take one step at a time.' I think that's a much more realistic picture about mission, than thinking that you can define it for life. For example, I started out as a chemical engineer at MIT, and I switched to be a physicist at Harvard. Then I went into the ministry and now I'm an author. So at various times in my life, I've seen my mission in different ways. Use what you know of your current mission as the compass to guide you in everything you do. Find out what your mission is this year, or this decade in your life, knowing that this may change."

My father changed careers three times. He was a dentist in private practice for 25 years; became a corporate officer and pioneered the dental insurance division of a major insurance company for 15 years; and in his retirement, was the lay leader of the synagogue in his community for 13 years, which brought him full circle with his Jewish studies from childhood. My father said, "Don't limit your horizons because you have skills you may not even be aware of until your forced to use them. Then you have to be smart enough to recognize that you have them." And that he did.

As your mission changes, be prepared for tests along the way "Adversity has the effect of eliciting talents which, in prosperous circumstances, would have lain dormant," wrote Horace in 20 BC. There is a risk in being successful and making changes. My father said, "It might seem like a disadvantage when you do not achieve your first goal, but talents accumulated by achieving various goals are never lost. In this way it is possible to accomplish much more in life than if you achieved one goal."

During a discussion with my husband Antonio about life's tests, he had this insight and said, "We are given challenges to see if we really believe what we say we do. If we listen, we will get reminders that the presence of God is there with us. We get a nudge to see if we've been paying attention. I compare it to the two-year old who wants to be independent but doesn't play long without checking back in with mom. We need to apply what we've learned, then trust and surrender."

A large part of the change and growth process is learning new skills and or finding new ways to reach our goals. Spencer Johnson, M.D. and author of the bestselling book, *Who Moved My Cheese?* writes about the styles of four mice who have to adapt to the cheese being moved. The message is that those of us who perceive that change is coming and prepare for it, adapt most quickly to change. Those who become angry or deny that change has arrived and do nothing, do not adapt well to change and pay the consequences. Those who eventually adapt to the change have to work through their denial and procrastination in order to see that there is something better.

A guest on my radio program, David Harder, author of *The Truth About Work: Making a Life and A Living* said, "Instead of saying, 'Well, I'd really like to change but I can't,' don't stop there! One of the major changes that has occurred in our world is that we can secure an enormous amount of information and education in such a short period of time. We can make changes in our lives much more quickly than we did just fifteen years ago. So we may not have the answer today, but if we know that we need and want to change our livelihood, we can get help, such as education or coaching. We're literally surrounded in a world that's filled with information and all we have to do is take the initiative to reach out for it."

Computer technology has brought change to all us. Those of us who have adapted the quickest to new technology have not only reaped the benefits of easier and faster communication, but have had an easier time with the ever changing modalities. I have received tremendous benefits from new technology while writing this book. I have been able to e-mail each chapter to my publisher, put additions in bold and make deletions in cross-out mode. This has saved so much time and paper and would not have been possible even five years ago. My book writing process has been practically paperless!

On the business side of positive career changes, Ivan Misner, Ph.D., co-author of New York Times Best-Selling *Masters of Networking* and the founder and CEO of BNI, Business Network International, the largest business networking organization in the world, talked about the GAINS Exchange on my radio program. The Exchange uses technology to help build business referrals. He said "GAINS is an acronym which stands for Goals, Accomplishments, Interests, Networks and Skills. If you want to get to know people well so that you can refer them, you really need to interview them so you can remember them. One of the beautiful things about technology today is that we can have databases with information on the people we want to work with. In the GAINS exchange, you go into the relationship openly and explain to the person that you want to learn about them personally and professionally and have them learn about you. We have a little form in the book that virtually walks through those acronyms. This is the idea of 'Givers Gain.' The idea is that if you give business to people and you give referrals to other people, you'll get in return. It's a philosophy of positive change that I believe in."

On the personal side of change, the computer enables us to reach out and touch family and friends, as well as learn new skills and hobbies. It gives us the easiest, fastest and cheapest way to stay in touch through e-mail. "There are now more e-mail messages than telephone calls. According to a report by International Data Corporation, by 2000, the volume of e-mail had reached 9.7 billion and the report predicts it will reach 34.6 billion by 2005," says Sandy Berger, guest on my radio program and author of *How to Have A Meaningful Relationship With You're Computer, Your Official Grown-ups Guide to AOL and the Internet* and *Sandy Berger's Cyber Savers.*

E-mail has created a positive, quiet revolution, which brings us efficiency in the rapid pace of technology. On my radio program, Sandy told of an older woman she helped to access the Internet so that she could communicate with her six children and eleven grandchildren who are spread out across the country. "Her son decided to move to Japan, and that's when she decided not to pay for long distance phone bills. By pressing one button on the mouse, she could send the same E-mail message to all eleven grandchildren. She did that one afternoon, and by the next morning she had eleven return messages. Now they call her 'Cyber-granny.'"

In *Time Wars,* author Jeremy Rifkin writes, "We are living longer and the computer is allowing us to cross all generational barriers. The computer and the Internet bring us many opportunities to learn, share and create bonds with our children and grandchildren, while helping us to exercise our mind which, as we age, is so important." My father at 85, corresponds with our family and his friends through e-mail. As we craft our messages, we are bringing "high-tech" and "high-touch" together.

There are spiritual gifts from this technology so well stated by John Naisbitt and Patricia Aburdene, authors of *Megatrends 2000.* "In telecommunications, we are moving to a single worldwide information network, just as economically we are becoming one global marketplace. We are moving toward the capability to communicate anything to anyone, anywhere, by any form – voice, data, text, or image – at the speed of light." As we expand our consciousness into this global dimension, we are brought closer to the unifying principle of commonality – the thread of oneness that runs through all of us.

# *Lead Others*

*Never tell people how to do things. Tell them what to do and they will surprise you with their ingenuity.* (General George S. Patton)

*G*iven a little direction, a few resources, elbow room and plenty of respect, most people will achieve incredible results. General Patton knew the secret to effective leadership: ask highly-talented people to do something meaningful, provide the resources they need, and then get out of their way. Leading others involves trusting people, respecting their time and talents and providing an environment that fosters their creativity and interest.

David Kyle, Ph.D. organizational consultant and author of *The Four Powers of Leadership,* and guest on my radio program captures the essence of leadership. He said: "Leadership is something one develops and grows into, not something one is born or trained to do. In my view, being a leader is not about acting out a role, but rather about accessing the power to maximize one's unique and individual capacities and potential. Leading is not primarily about doing something, but rather about being something. The development of leadership is about becoming conscious of both the power within oneself and the power inherent within the position one holds."

Dr. Kyle outlined six leadership qualities that make powerful and successful leaders. They are: 1) They learn to reflect on themselves. 2) They learn to see into and beyond what others see around them in the conditions and situations of their environment. 3) They learn to focus less on themselves and more on the people who are attracted to working with them. 4) They gain perspective on and develop humility regarding the depth of their innate capabilities. 5) They

130

continually attempt to access other hidden parts of themselves, which, in turn engenders a fuller capacity for leadership. Finally, 6) These leaders discover that leading is a practice to be worked on every day.

Brooke Astor writes "Power is the ability to do good things for others." My father illustrates the spirit of leadership in this adaptation of a biblical story:

> *The children of Israel are in the desert. God takes the spirit of leadership and puts it over seventy elders to help Moses lead. Two decline the honor of using the spirit given to them by God, but they begin prophesizing in the camp. Joshua, second in command, comes to Moses and tells him to stop them because he fears that the honor and authority of Moses is being diminished by these two who have received the spirit through Moses and do not use it. The other elders feel that only Moses should be their leader. Moses says, 'Are you jealous for my sake? I wish that of all of the children of Israel to whom God put his spirit of prophecy.' God gave Moses respect to bring everyone up to his level. A true leader is never threatened by competition as this story points out. How much better this world would be if more people took positive leadership roles and lead rather than follow.*

Leadership can start right at home and applies to our family life especially when teaching our children. Helping our children work together as team players, make good decisions at an early age, use critical thinking skills to see others' viewpoints, set the stage for leadership. In my work as a guidance counselor years ago, I used the S.T.E.P. program, which stands for Systematic Training for Effective Parenting based on Adlerian Psychology, to lead parenting groups. The program was based on teaching children responsibility, self-reliance, cooperation, mutual respect and self-esteem. One of the strongest components of the program is the concept of the family meeting where families would get together weekly to outline responsibilities, share ideas, discuss concerns, and plan family events. Leadership isn't reserved for our work life. It's part of everything we do.

Leading others – at work, at home, in a volunteer setting or during fun outings – is about getting things done through people. It's about tapping their skills, talents and abilities to move toward collective outcomes. Effective leadership helps turn ordinary people into extraordinary performers. The key lies in the example of the leader.

Tim McCullen, President of The Window Gang, talked about how important leadership and training is in to success. "All of our franchisees are trained how to wash a house and windows and we always keep them up to date on new procedures and products and constantly stay in touch. Our goal now is to make our franchises more successful. If I help others succeed, then I ultimately succeed. I feel personal success when we're building other people's success and I am so happy when they do well. It's so exciting to me when a franchisee uses my plan, follows it and it works for him. It's just great!"

Perhaps the essence of leadership is best described by Dr. Bil Holton in his award-winning book, *The Manager's Short Course to a Long Career*, which he co-authored with his wife, Dr. Cher Holton. He says, "Leadership builds trust – that special dimension which assures those who follow that the one who leads will always act morally, guaranteeing the wellness of each individual. A sense of rightness surrounds the mysterious and charismatic qualities of leadership. A leader's essence is punctuated with uncompromised integrity."

The fundamental message here is that family, friends and colleagues respect leaders who – like Moses – can take care of them, honor individual differences and model the same kind of behavior they expect from others.

## *Positive Pollination*

*List:*

* ❖ Your talents and abilities which are relative to your life purpose.
* ❖ The P's to success you use.
* ❖ Your latest, favorite expenditure and the value it represents.
* ❖ The last change you made for the better.
* ❖ An example of what you do when you lead others at home, in social situations, or at work.

*Reflect on:*

* ❖ Your life's purpose.
* ❖ How you apply the 5 P's to success.
* ❖ How your talents and skills relate to your work.
* ❖ How you align your money and your values.
* ❖ How adaptable you are to change and how you respond to change.
* ❖ Situations where you lead others.
* ❖ How often you have "advanced confidently" in the direction of your dreams.

## CHAPTER FIVE

# Focus on the Positive

*Life inflicts the same setbacks and tragedies on the optimist as on the pessimist, but the optimist weathers them better.* (Martin E. P. Seligman)

*P*sychologists have estimated that the average person has over 62,000 thoughts each day. Most people's thoughts are a hodgepodge of internal concerns about money, sex, work, rent, car payments, meals, TV programming, health care, grocery lists, family issues, child rearing, the economy and traffic. Those 62,000 thoughts usually center around ordinary activities and responsibilities that fill our daily lives.

Most people don't think about how many thoughts power their day. They don't keep track of the kind of thoughts they have – whether they're positive or negative, fleeting or introspective, directed or unrelated to what they are doing. Most people have no real appreciation for the amount of internal dialogue that hums constantly in their brains.

Unfortunately, most of the mental chatter is negative, because most of us grow up in negative environments. Our school, church and family environments are built on negative messages like, "Don't do this" and "Don't do that." Our work environments reinforce that pessimism by hammering negative messages at us like, "Don't rock the boat," and "That will never work here."

Negative perspectives serve an important function when it comes to seeking clarity and direction. However, when negation takes over as the controlling element in the thinking process and dominates the thinking itself, it becomes divisive and self-defeating. Negative thinkers look for negative outcomes, accept negative outcomes and create negative outcomes.

This chapter focuses on the other half of the thinking process – the positive side, the side that says, "Think positively. Believe that good triumphs." As William James, the great American philosopher and psychologist said, "The greatest discovery of my generation is that human beings can alter their lives by altering their attitudes and they can alter their attitudes by altering their thinking." His wisdom applies to any generation.

He fully understood the power of both positive and negative thinking. William James preferred to think positively. He believed that good triumphs, and so do I. So let's take a look at the power of positive thinking and its ability to generate positive outcomes, outcomes based on the belief that good always triumphs.

# *Find Sources of Positive Inspiration*

*When you are inspired by some great purpose, some extraordinary project, all your thoughts break their bonds; your mind transcends limitations, your consciousness expands in every direction, and you find yourself in a new, great and wonderful world.* (Patanjoli)

*T*he achievements of ordinary people who accomplish extraordinary things inspire us. Touched by someone's incredible feat, we feel energized. Something inside us says, 'I may do something special, too.' Patanjoli also says, "Dormant forces within us cause certain faculties and talents to come alive." Things we thought impossible fall within the realm of possibility.

For twenty years, I have been interviewing people who have shared inspiring stories. They come from all walks of life, but they have one thing in common: they were inspired by someone. In every case, my guests report they began their own quest – or renewed their commitment – for personal and professional fulfillment when they witnessed the accomplishments of someone who excelled in a similar field of interest.

On one of my programs, I asked Linda Sivertsen, author of *Lives Charmed: Intimate Conversations with Extraordinary People*, if writing the book had made her life more charmed. She responded, "I was amazed at how my life has shifted through knowing powerful people. It's so exciting when you are around people who love what they are doing and feel that they are contributing worthwhile accomplishments. There is a celebration of life in those people that rubs off on you. Being around them has made me realize that one person really can make a big difference."

Simple actions can make a big difference, too. Jim Carey, famous comedian and actor, wrote a check in the amount he desired to be paid many years before he actually received it. He believed in the power of suggestion and turned his positive attitude into a tangible action which reminded him every day to work toward the income he desired. Sometimes actions like Jim Carey's seem ridiculous or fanciful, but they are positive statements of internal beliefs. And when people are able to turn wishful thinking into *wishcraft* and accomplish the impossible, they inspire us. They remind us that we, too, can achieve something we thought was impossible.

Lynda Dahl, co-author of *The Book of Fallacies: A Little Primer of New Thought,* says, "We have far more flexibility in our lives than we have ever dreamed possible. Because of the field of probabilities and the innate purpose to our lives, we are surrounded by possibilities of great significance. Our lives can expand in numerous directions, some that we haven't even identified yet, if we truly understand the power of our thoughts to create our lives along lines of conscious choice."

When ice skater Sarah Hughes was interviewed after her amazing Olympic gold medal performance in Salt Lake City, she told Scott Hamilton she had been inspired by the great figure skaters over the past ten years, including the phenomenally-talented Michelle Kwan, who she outskated for the Olympic gold medal. "Ever since I was six years old, I wanted to skate like Kristi (Yamaguchi), Tara (Lipinski) and Michelle (Kwan). I saw myself winning a gold medal at the Olympics," Sarah confirmed.

The sources of inspiration for Sara were national record holders, world champion figure skaters and coaches who epitomized her ideals in women's figure skating. She was inspired by parents and friends who believed in her. Sarah's spirited performance inspired others and it's a great example of how inspiration works.

Hundreds of young girls, barely able to stand on skates, flock to gymnasiums across America so they can be like Sarah Hughes, who at age sixteen is one of the youngest figure skating champions in Olympic history and the only woman skater to land two triple-triple jump combinations in competition as of this writing.

On Positive Living, two of my guests were John Groom, publisher of Positive Press, a web site that collects positive news stories, and Jon Wilson, editor and publisher of HOPE magazine, which is based on *people who make a difference.* Both men feel the media should pay more attention to the positive news. "There's an overabundance of negative news," John Wilson reported. "What we need is a strong positive media medium." John Groom agreed, "The world is better than what the negative media portrays. People are better than this...There are values out there that need a fair hearing."

It was so uplifting for me, personally, to have these two kindred spirits on Positive Living. I recently spoke with a physician who told me that his journalist daughter tells him there's a saying in the media, "If it doesn't bleed, it doesn't lead," which means if a story is not sensational, it won't make the front page. I would rephrase that adage to read, "If it doesn't feed, it shouldn't lead," meaning that if it doesn't nourish our positive beliefs, it shouldn't be the focus of media coverage. Think about what would happen if television and newspapers focused on positive stories of human achievements instead of negative behaviors and events.

In 1982 I began the journey of bringing positive stories to the forefront as an independent producer. I have continued to stay true to my belief and mission in the power of positive stories. In the introduction from my first book,

*Success Your Dream and You*, I state, "The answer to so many questions has been 'think positively.' And yet, it is just that effort to be positive in our thoughts and purpose that enables us to create the results we want.

## *Choose Role Models Carefully*

*There are two ways of spreading light: to be the candle or the mirror that reflects it.*
(Edith Warton)

*I* believe that in order to achieve a new behavior or value, you must find appropriate role models, and spend time with them. I'm talking about watching behavior as well as taking in information using all five senses, including what you see, hear, touch, smell and taste. When your mind and body are working together, you will move in the direction of what you ultimately want. 'Birds of a feather flock together' really rings true for me. Think about how you feel after you've been in one of these special places. When you find these places and people that move you deeply, stay with them.

Chris Prentiss, a dynamic guest on my radio program, is the author of *The Little Book of Secrets: 81 Secrets for Living a Happy, Prosperous and Successful Life*, which is based on the philosophy of the *I Ching*.

He explains, "Certain people uplift us; others pull us down. Certain people give us strength; others drain our energy. We must choose carefully. Good friends, like good neighbors are an endless benefit. Bad relationships can ruin a lifetime. Following the path of a knowledgeable, successful person permits a sort of natural selection that retrofits us only with the best quality friends."

My husband, Antonio, and I interviewed Drs. Renee and Kimberly O'Sullivan on "Plastic Surgery Today." Antonio asked me to co-host this program with him and it was a fascinating interview. The O'Sullivans are a mother/daughter plastic surgery team. Dr. Renee O'Sullivan was the only board-certified female plastic surgeon in New England for many years. In addition to that challenging role, she was also a single mother, raising three daughters, who all went on to become physicians – two plastic surgeons and a dermatologist. I asked her daughter, Dr. Kimberly O'Sullivan, if her mom encouraged her to be a plastic surgeon.

*"Well, I wouldn't say that she encouraged me to be a plastic surgeon directly," Dr. Kimberly O'Sullivan admitted, "but she loves what she does so much and she has such an enthusiastic and positive attitude towards everything she does that I think I gravitated toward it naturally. We would come home from school and help in the office, meet patients, file and assist her on little procedures. She loved what she did so much and the patients loved her so much that it was hard to imagine any other profession. I always knew I wanted to become a doctor."*

*On her mother's impact in her life, she said, "My mother was such a positive role model," Never wonderful. Never once did she say we could never do that. Any time we had an interest she just encouraged us to pursue that interest, which is quite different from a lot of people whose parents say, 'Oh, you'd never be able to do that,' or 'Oh, you wouldn't function if you did that,' or 'You're not good enough.'"*

141

*"You didn't have many role models, did you?" I asked Dr. Renee O'Sullivan.*

*"Most of the time people were saying, 'Oh you can't do that and you won't be able to raise a family if you are a surgeon,'" she responded.*

Dr. Renee O'Sullivan is not only a role model for her daughters, she is an inspiration for any woman who values character, vision and family ties. Every one of us has our own image of success. As we move toward that image, we must separate the wheat role models from the chaff role models. Each one of us is our own Christopher Columbus, charting the life ahead of us and hoping we stay on course. Choosing the right role models to help steer our course is essential to our success.

# *Pay Attention to Logical Consequences*

*What goes around, comes around.*
(American proverb)

*A*s a guidance counselor, I studied psychology, specifically the *S.T.E.P.* (Systematic Training for Effective Parenting) *Program* by Don Dinkmeyer, which I mentioned in Chapter 4. Based on the principles of Dr. Alfred Adler, the *S.T.E.P.* concept teaches children lessons from the "natural and logical consequences" of their actions. For example, if a child does not listen to a parent's repeated warnings to stop acting in such a way that might embarrass or annoy someone, the parent does not intervene the next time the recalcitrant child disobeys. This allows the child to experience the consequences of his or her actions.

The following childhood experience taught me the concept of "logical consequences" long before I incorporated it into my work.

*It was a summer day and I was an energetic ten-year old. My father and I were driving to our beach cottage and passed several ice cream stands on our way. I asked my father to stop so I could have some ice cream. This happened twice without incident. The third time I asked, he told me I had had enough. But when I persisted, he stopped and bought me a third cone. When I asked for two dips, he hesitated, but bought me what I wanted. A short while later I said, "Daddy, I don't want anymore ice cream. I think I'm sick."*

*That incident has stayed with me all these years. Learning the consequences of one's actions is an important life lesson. My father knew what effect six scoops of ice cream would have on me. He was also wise enough to know that his ten-year-old daughter would have to find out for herself. My father knew I would have a stomachache, but he felt that this was an important lesson, and indeed it was. Self-control and moderation are essential for living a balanced, healthy and purposeful life. Every action has its consequences. The message is the same for children as well as adults.*

Consequences are the effects of actions and reactions are the effects of consequences. One of my guests, Betty J. Eadie, author of *The Ripple Effect, Our Harvest,* says that every act has consequences that go well beyond those we experience personally. The choices we make every day ripple into the lives of those around us. "We live in an energy field," she says. "When we think positive thoughts, positive energy ripples out to others and helps them to be more at ease and more peaceful. The reverse is true as well. When we have negative thoughts or we do negative deeds, those ripples are also felt by other people. Our actions are *things* that we create and everything that we create ripples out. We interrelate with each other just like pieces of a puzzle."

## *Visualize Positive Outcomes*

*There is a law in psychology that if you form a picture in your mind of what you would like to be, and you keep that picture there long enough, you will soon become exactly as you have been thinking.* (William James)

*V*isualizing positive outcomes is using your imagination to create what you want in your mind's eye. I have used visualization techniques for many years, and I can tell you that the power of your "mental movies" to change your life is real, enriching and life-affirming. The stuff that dreams are made of is the stuff we visualize and believe can happen.

Shakti Gwain, author of the inspirational bestseller *Creative Visualization*, says that you can "use your imagination in a more and more conscious way, as a technique to create what you truly want." She goes on to say that creative visualization gives us "a key to tap into the natural goodness and bounty of life." As scientists now know from biofeedback technology, we can alter our heart rate and other functions through the process of visualization. Researchers are rediscovering how much our outer experience is connected to our inner experience.

"These movies-of-the-mind," says Adelaide Bry, author of *Visualization: Directing the Movies of Your Mind*, "help improve your health, expand your thinking and achieve goals you wouldn't otherwise believe you could." When you visualize, you bypass the limitations of your rational, logical, linear mind and tap into the limitless source of your creative, intuitive, left brain. On a practical level, this means your right brain consciousness does not know the difference between wishful thinking and reality. So, when you visualize – a right-brain process – your subconscious mind *believes* the mental images you project are part of your physical reality. This is why it is so important to visualize positive outcomes. Your subconscious will believe negative images as well.

Visual imaging is a process that takes time and patience, but it is time well spent. My father points out that "The Bible says to ask, believing you have received, and it shall be given unto you; that whatever you wish to accomplish must be totally and firmly implanted within your mind." This implanting begins the day you are born, and you continue to add footage to these mental movies each time you think, act and visualize.

A considerable amount of research suggests that the images we hold for ourselves become self-fulfilling prophecies. That statement may be the most important statement in this book. Whatever we experience in our lives – whether we see it as happy or sad, good or bad, justified or unjustified – is the result of our mental images. According to Dr. John Lilly, "What we believe to be true in our mind becomes true in physical reality."

When you want to reinforce your highest thoughts, place yourself in an environment that is conducive to effecting them. Neal Donald Welsh in his best selling book, *Conversations with God*, says that by "thinking our highest thoughts, we are serving God." That really struck me because I realized how simple that sounds, and how difficult it is to do. Then I wondered what the world would be like if everyone always thought their highest thoughts. What if we always visualize positive outcomes? Suppose we *saw* everything in a positive light?

When you visualize positive outcomes, make your mental pictures as clear, specific and real as you can. Form in your mind a precise image of what you need, imagine how good it will feel to have what you need, and then put the images out of your mind for a while. Play the mental movie several times each day. Visualize the same positive outcome. Replay those images as often as you can until they become real. It may take weeks, months or even years to turn mental images into physical reality, but that is how the imaging process works. It takes commitment, patience, practice and most of all, belief in the power of positive imaging and trust in the process.

In my book, *Success, Your Dreams and You*, I wrote: "The answer to so many of life's questions is to think positively. It is the effort to hold positive thoughts, regardless of the appearances of outer circumstances, that enables us to create the future we want...And that future comes from the inner pictures we create in our visions...It's the stuff dreams are made of." Even though I wrote that ten years ago, it still rings true today. Our search for answers is the search for selfhood, and that search for selfhood means all of us are in the same soul awareness business: pathfinding.

# *Tune Into the Highest Frequency*

*Beauty, truth, friendship, love, creation? These*
*are the great values of life. We can't prove them,*
*or explain them, yet they are the most stable*
*things in our lives.*          (Jesse Herman Holmes)

*I* work with Taylor Hyman, a very special woman who is trained in reflexology (foot massage). She often greets me by telling me how good I look or how she sees brightness in my eyes. Taylor will often tell me it is an honor and privilege to work with me. During my reflexology sessions, I feel that she is watering my creativity and nurturing my abilities. She combines her expertise with kindness and appreciation and her reflexology practice is an extension of her goodness. Taylor has a generous heart and a nurturing soul. She has an intuitive sense of her clients' needs, and we all feel her love and energy.

John Randolph Price, renowned teacher and author, of *Super Beings* and other spiritual books, talks about how kindness is a higher vibrational energy, and that when we move up in vibrational frequency, we move up in life. He says that everything is energy and that energy follows thought. What we focus on grows. An example of this is the story of "The Hundredth Monkey" phenomenon:

*In 1952, on the island of Koshima scientists were feeding monkeys sweet potatoes dropped in the sand. The monkeys loved the sweet potatoes, but found the gritty sand unpleasant.*

*An 18-month old female named Imo solved the problem by washing the potatoes in a nearby stream. She taught this trick to her family.*

*Between 1952 and 1958, all the young monkeys followed Imo's lead and learned to wash the sandy sweet potatoes to make them more palatable. Only the adults who imitated their children learned this social improvement. Other adults stuck in the old ways continued eating the dirty sweet potatoes.*

*Then something amazing happened. In the autumn of 1958, a certain number of Koshima monkeys were washing sweet potatoes – the exact number is not known. Legend has it that when the sun rose one morning, there were 99 monkeys on Koshima Island who had learned to wash their sweet potatoes. Later that morning, the inevitable happened. The hundredth monkey learned to wash potatoes.*

*By that evening almost every monkey in the tribe washed the sweet potatoes before eating them. The added energy of the "hundredth monkey" somehow created an ideological breakthrough, where washing the sweet potatoes became a cultural behavior rather than an individual choice!*

*The scientists observed an amazing thing. The habit of washing sweet potatoes jumped over the sea. Colonies of monkeys on other islands and the mainland tribe of monkeys at Takasakiyama, began washing their sweet potatoes.*

It appears that when a certain critical number achieves a new awareness, this new awareness may be communicated from mind to mind. Although the exact number may vary, the "hundredth monkey phenomenon" suggests that there is a point at which if only one more person tunes-in to a new awareness, a field is strengthened so that this awareness is absorbed by many more people, almost simultaneously.

One of my father's stories expresses this concept so wonderfully:

*During World War II, I found myself stationed at Christmas Island in the Pacific for a short period of time. It so happened that it was the time of Jewish High Holy Days. I was leading the services in a little grass shack with open sides that served as a chapel. It seated about fifty people and we had about fifteen Jewish attendees.*

*Towards the conclusion of the service, I looked up and there to my astonishment were about fifty natives who sat in the chapel and several dozen more standing outside looking in. They appeared to be interested and respectful. After the service was over, I asked their leader if he understood the service. He said he did not, but was told by the missionaries that whenever there was a service in the chapel, it was good and they should attend.*

When my father told me the story, he pointed out what a beautiful thing it was for people to attend a religious ceremony without knowing or understanding what it was they were listening to. He said, "These people were seeking the spirituality of a religious service. If they could feel a warmth and spiritual uplift from something they didn't understand, think about how much easier it is for knowledgeable people to get a spiritual uplift when they surround themselves with people who practice loving kindness and brotherly love."

This high frequency of energy is contagious. When I think about "the hundredth monkey effect," I realize how much energy we transfer when we learn, model and take action. When we are immersed in positive energy, we can tell immediately when something does not feel right, and it becomes much easier to make the right choices. We can find positive energy in a variety of ways, from being in the garden, to walking in the woods or on the beach, to spending time with a friend. Even special possessions, such as a pin, piece of crystal, a plate, a charm bracelet or grandmother's shawl, can give positive energy. Those are the things we need to surround ourselves with.

Search until you find the people and things that resonate with you like a tuning fork, and you are saying to yourself, 'I really love this,' 'It was so wonderful to be with that person today,' or 'Going to that place did so much for me.' Then you know you are on that high frequency of positive energy.

# *Practice Self-Care*

*The fate and character of each of us is born in mystery, and our individuality is so profound and so hidden that it (could) take (an) entire lifetime for identity to emerge. (Self-care) is the ability to give ordinary life the depth, meaning and value that come with soulfulness.*

(Thomas Moore)

he high frequency that positive energy brings is especially powerful when practicing self-care. A Chinese acupuncturist once said to me, "The body doesn't lie." No matter what you read, no matter what your physicians tell you, you ultimately are the master of your own health. You know how you feel and your body talks to you. The signals are always there.

On Positive Living, guest Marcia Hutchinson, author of *200 Ways to Love the Body You Have*, discussed how to be more self-aware and centered in your body.

When I asked her how to begin to love the body you have she said, "It's important to develop a relationship where you become aware of the dance that's going on all the time in your body, such as paying attention to the gurgling in your stomach, or feeling the tension in your shoulders and then use that somatic information in your self-care."

In her first book, *Transforming Body Image: Love the Body You Have*, Ms. Hutchinson writes, "One of the main casualties in your mind/body struggle is your body itself. All bodies need proper care to maintain good physical health. Movement and exercise are important, but proper exercise requires a real caring for the body. It requires a program of movement performed with loving sensitivity as a gift, not as a punishment for wayward flesh."

On the show she added, "If you go to the gym out of a sense of guilt, you would workout differently than if you went because you wanted to be able to develop a finely-tuned body awareness. It's a different experience with a very different result. Acceptance means acknowledging where you are and who you are. It means accepting the fact that the body you have is the body you have. It is not the same as resignation where you despairingly give in and give up. Acceptance gives you the potential to move beyond where you are. It's a paradox. To change something in ourselves, we must first accept ourselves as we are."

One of the key elements in pathfinding is persistence and persistence requires stamina. If you have not added self-care to your pathfinding regimen, you may deplete your energies before you reach your goals. Ignoring your health and nutritional needs is not a good pathfinding strategy.

On Positive Living several years ago, I interviewed Dr. Lester Sauvage, a world-renowned heart surgeon, researcher, and author of *You Can Beat Heart Disease* and *The Open Heart.* The program was dedicated to the memory of Terry Barts, youth pastor at Glad Tidings Pentecostal Holiness Church, who transformed thousands of teenagers and adults with his positive, down-to-earth messages.

On the program, Dr. Sauvage talked about five cardinal rules for healthy living that are discussed extensively in *You Can Beat Heart Disease.* The letters SDEWS represent the five rules. **S** stands for *smoking.* Dr. Sauvage said, "Smoking accelerates the development of hardening of the arteries and severely damages elastic tissues in the lungs causing emphysema."

The letter **D** is for *diet.* Dr. Sauvage referred to the "better life diet." He says that 50 percent of our calories should come from high fiber foods; 30 percent from fat, especially protective fats that are liquid at room temperature, such as olive oil; and 20 percent should come from protein. "But most importantly," he states, "you must reduce the refined sugar in your diet – honey and brown and white sugar. The average individual eats 150 pounds of sugar per year. That's 38 percent of the calories in an ordinary diet. Most of this sugar ends up as fat inside your blood vessels."

**E** stands for *exercise*. Dr. Sauvage states, "Exercise is vital. It's good for you both psychologically and physically. The best form of exercise for the vast majority of people is walking a couple of miles briskly everyday."

**W** represents *weight*. Our best weight is the weight we feel and look the best at.

The last letter is **S**, which stands for *stress*. Dr. Sauvage believes, "Stress kills. Stress is our reaction to what's outside of us. It can cause the adrenal gland to produce lots of adrenaline, which causes blood vessels to constrict, makes the heart work a lot harder, elevates pressure and produces platelets in the blood which cause clotting, heart attacks and strokes."

What Dr. Sauvage is telling us is that we've got to pay attention to ourselves, mentally and physically. Two keys to self-management are self-care and self-observation. It is important to realize that self-observation is not the same thing as over-criticism or judgmentalism. It takes consistent self-monitoring. Self-monitoring, it seems, is tied to good health, and good health is tied to self-care. "To lose one's health," says Herophilus, "renders science null, art inglorious, strength unavailing, wealth useless and elegance powerless." Health is precious. Without it you won't be able to go very far down any path, and in particular the path toward selfhood.

## *Live Well to Age Well*

*It is magnificent to grow old, if one keeps
young.*  (Harry Emerson Fosdick)

*L*iving well is a prerequisite to aging well. The attitudes, values, beliefs and habits we cultivate in our youth and early adulthood are usually reinforced throughout our lives. If we're an old, opinionated sourpuss, it's probably because we were a young one. If we're an old procrastinator, we were most likely a young procrastinator. If we work out, jog and swim in old age, it's likely we disciplined ourselves in those activities as a young man or woman. "To know how to grow old," says Henri F. Amiel in his famous *Journal*, "is a masterwork of wisdom, and one of the most difficult chapters in the great art of living."

Some people see aging as a time to live more quietly, away from the hustle and bustle of career and family responsibilities. They see it as a time to prepare for retirement and death. Many people, however, are embracing the second half of life. "Old age is not a disease – it is strength and survivorship, triumph over all kinds of vicissitudes and disappointments, trials and illnesses," says Maggie Kuhn, founder of the Gray Panthers, an elderly activism organization. According to the founder, "What I've especially liked about getting old is that it's a miracle to be able to tap into the incredible energy of young people, while making use of the knowledge and experience that comes after living a long, full life."

In her book, *The Essential Grandparent: A Guide to Making a Difference*, one of my guests, Dr. Lillian Carson, talks about how grandparenting is a key to aging well. On the program she said, "Grandparenting well is a key to aging well, because being in touch with the young keeps us young. It is really our natural task to nurture the young and to be involved with the young. Seeing the wisdom of the world through a child's eyes enhances our immune system, energizes us, and keeps us aware of things that we may not ordinarily notice. It truly is important for us to honor this by being an involved grandparent."

Dr. Diana Schwarzbein, couldn't agree more. Dr. Schwarzbein was a guest on Positive Living. An endocrinologist, she is a leading authority on metabolic healing, founder of The Endocrinology Institute of Santa Barbara and author of *The Schwarzbein Principle: The Truth About Losing Weight, Being Healthy and Feeling Younger.*

"The reason this book is called *The Schwarzbein Principle*," she explained, "is because the principle is that degenerative diseases of aging are acquired and not genetic. This is a bold statement to point out that 90 percent of what happens to us, health-wise, is due to our daily habits. Now that we are living long enough to fall apart, it is more important than ever to take care of ourselves.

Dr. Schwarzbein talked about the effects of accelerated metabolic aging and how we now see the diseases of old age in much younger individuals. She said, "Your cells have a cellular age that cannot be changed, and a metabolic age that can be changed. We age and die. We just want to do it as gracefully as we can." In order to accomplish this, Dr. Schwarzbein has devised a five-step lifestyle program that encompasses healthy eating, tapering off chemicals, exercise, stress management and hormone replacement therapy.

She states, "Eat real foods. Balance proteins, healthy fats, non-starchy vegetables, and carbohydrates at every meal. Never skip meals, stay away from chemicals. Exercise, take time out and do something nice for yourself daily. Take HRT (hormone replacement therapy) if necessary." According to Dr. Schwarzbein, these are common sense things that will keep your hormones balanced and slow down the accelerated aging process.

Another powerful source of information comes from Dr. Andrew Weil, who for many years has been at the forefront of information on healing and nutrition. His groundbreaking books have helped millions to feel better, live longer and avoid illness by integrating the best of modern medicine and natural healing practices.

The whole subject of positive aging has been a passion of mine because for twenty years now, I have had a strong premonition that I will live until I am at least 100 years old. I read a book about the Hunzas, who have the longest centenarian success rate. They live at very high altitudes, eat the food they grow off the land, and walk many miles a day. How we can extend our years of life and at the same time maintain our quality of life has always fascinated me. I found older, positive role models when I was producing "Positive Aging in North Carolina," a documentary for the North Carolina Division of Aging, which aired on the North Carolina PBS affiliate several years ago.

*One of the people I featured in that documentary was Harley Potter from Winston-Salem, North Carolina. At that time, he was a 102-year-old golfer who had won gold medals at local, state and national tournaments. His 73-year-old daughter, Leta Duffin drove him to our on-location shoot and rode in the golf cart with him. Harley's only major impairment was the 25 percent hearing he had left in one ear, so we would direct the questions to that ear. This man was as happy as he could be as long as he had a golf club in his hand. Harley said, "You are never to old to learn to play golf. I started when I was 92, and I never had a lesson." On his golf game, Harley said, "My handicap was 44 when I started, but now it's down to 37. The last game I played, my score was 100."*

*I asked Harley his secret to long life. He said, "I don't worry. Yesterday is gone and there is nothing you can do about it today. I look forward to today and beyond that, I keep going. I watch my health. I've never smoked. I eat three meals a day, but never eat too much and I exercise. His daughter, Leta, told me, "Daddy never thought of himself as being very old. He always figured that you were only as old as you acted. So he did a lot of things. He sang in the church choir. He never felt he shouldn't be singing at the age of 100. Daddy died peacefully at 106 after being in a nursing home for about two years."*

*I asked Leta what her father taught her. She said, "He taught me not to worry about tomorrow or about the past. Daddy didn't teach me by telling me. He taught me by living it."*

*Leta recounted her nine-year-old granddaughter, Elizabeth's experience with her father, "Daddy loved for Elizabeth to visit him when he was in the nursing home. She would visit him often and wheel him out into the park. Everyone knew when she was coming, because Daddy would come rushing down the hall-way to meet us. Elizabeth loved him dearly and one of the most beautiful things she did during the funeral was to put a tiny pink glass heart inside his pocket in his casket."*

When I shared Harley Potter's story with my father, he commented, "I hope I can make it to 106. I realize I'll have to watch my diet, exercise more often and watch my lifestyle habits. I wonder, though, what difference it really makes whether one lives to be 90, 100 or 106? I want to keep living because I want to see both my children and grandchildren become successful. One could keep going until you ask yourself when is enough enough? When are you satisfied? To me, there is only one way to respond to its question. As Admiral Dewey once said, 'Damn the torpedoes! Full speed ahead!' I believe you've got to stay active and surround yourself with people who have positive outlooks."

I reflected on what my father told me and realized how much he followed his own advice. As he was being wheeled down to hall on the way to open heart surgery, he said to us, "We'll start again. We'll start from scratch. We'll take baby steps, but we'll take a lot of them!"

After fifty-eight years of marriage, my parents are great role models of strength, persistence and generosity. My father is on the local hospital board, and although retired as a lay rabbi, he still officiates at weddings and funerals and occasionally gives sermons at the synagogue. My mother is the past president of the local woman's club and is on the board of American Association of University Women and hospital auxiliary.

Dr. Mark Williams, Ward K. Ensminger distinguished professor of geriatric medicine, chief of the Division of General Medicine and Geriatrics at the University of Virginia Health System, and author of *Complete Guide to Aging and Health,* summed up in a positive way what happens to the body as we age. When he was a guest on "Perspective on Healthy Aging," a series I produced in the Piedmont region of North Carolina several years ago, Dr. Williams stated, "The body changes over time. We have a considerable amount of influence over those changes. Our intellect continues to grow and unfold. We solve problems very differently when we're young. In the area of psychology, there's a deepening of our awareness and of our sensibility. When we look at the totality of human experience, we become more and not less."

Recently, on Positive Living, I had the opportunity to interview Dr. Williams again. He discussed his four keys to positive aging which are: challenge your body, stimulate your intellect, manage your emotions and nurture your spirit.

On challenging the body Dr. Williams said, "Physical aging is not an inevitable downhill decline and we can control it through exercise, activity, diet, nutrition and a variety of things that keep us in physical health far longer than expected. In longitudinal studies of older people, people who are 75 years old today are biologically the equivalent of 65 years old in 1960. We're not only living longer, we're living better."

I asked about the relationship between longevity and our genetic background. Dr. Williams said, "Experts tell us that about 30 percent of our longevity is due to our genes. That implies 70 percent of our longevity depends on our environment and lifestyle choices.

Imagine a ski lift where our genetic endowment gets us to the top of the hill. There, we can choose what kind of trip we want to take down the hill. We can either choose to go very quickly, take plenty of risks and perhaps have a short ride; or we can take our time and enjoy the scenery."

Dr. Williams' second key to positive aging is to stimulate our intellect. He said, "Plato once said that our spiritual eyesight improves as our physical eyesight declines. I think that it's important to appreciate that changes in our mental function are perhaps one of the most feared aspects in aging. Mental dysfunction threatens our lives and our independence. The good news is that for most people this fear of becoming mentally incompetent is groundless and that learning capacity really continues through life."

The third key to positive aging is managing our emotions. Dr. Williams said, "Stress can cause a number of illnesses. One of the laws of the universe says that conflict, stress and frustration equal expectations divided by reality.

When there's a difference between what we expect and what actually happens, conflict results. In my geriatric training, two elderly women taught me a great life lesson. They shared a room together in a nursing home and one of the women had a number of extended family members who would feed her breakfast every morning and her supper every evening. She was miserable and upset because she felt that someone should feed her lunch, as well. She felt her family was abandoning her despite giving her huge amounts of attention most of the day.

"Her roommate was a woman whose family visited on major holidays such as Easter and Christmas. She complained that they harassed her by visiting her too much," he continued. "She wished they would just leave her alone. Each of these women had different expectations. Neither of their expectations matched the reality of the situation."

On the fourth key to positive aging, nurturing our spirit, Dr. Williams said, "I think there are a number of very compelling aging statistics, but there's one that strikes very close to home: the death rate in this country is one per person per lifetime. The fact that we die is what gives meaning to the time that we have. Every moment is precious. The great mythologist, Joseph Campbell, used an analogy of the light bulb. Over time, the light bulb will physically age and eventually burn out. The light is produced by the bulb which is only the light's vehicle. The essence of nurturing our spirit, the light from the bulb, depends on how well we age."

For me, positive aging follows positive living. Quality of life is not dependent upon age. It's dependent upon how we live each day of our lives. I like to compare aging to fine wine that matures and improves with age. That's one of my life goals.

## *Positive Pollination*

*List:*
- ❖ Positive things that have happened to you today.
- ❖ Sources of inspiration in your life.
- ❖ Role models in your life.
- ❖ Outcomes you have experienced because you visualized them first.
- ❖ People, places and things that bring you laughter.
- ❖ People, places and things that bring you comfort, peace and joy.
- ❖ Elders in your life who inspire you.

*Reflect on:*
- ❖ How many positive thoughts power your day.
- ❖ How much of your "mental chatter" is negative programming.
- ❖ Your positive accomplishments.
- ❖ How your thinking and behavior affect your loved ones.
- ❖ How many of your childhood experiences helped form your concept of "logical consequences."

## CHAPTER SIX

# Protect and Respect
# Rewarding
# Relationships

*When people form interpersonal relationships, they must coordinate their mutual behaviors and adapt to one another...The relationship they form is the product of interdependence... although neither loses his or her identity. Each contributes to the quality and structure of the relationship.*

(Mark Steinberg)

*L*ife is about relationships and interrelationships. If you look deeply at any family, society or nation, you will find a universe of intricately woven interrelationships. We are all surrounded by networks of people, places and things that nurture the quality of our lives. That network may include family, friends, work associates, professional associations, religious groups or special support groups.

A growing body of research in clinical medicine and the social sciences confirms the life giving and life sustaining importance of positive relationships. Dean Ornish, MD, president and director of the Preventive Medicine Research Institute in Sausalito, California and bestselling author of four books says, "I'm coming to believe that anything that promotes isolation leads to chronic stress and in time may lead to illnesses like heart disease and cancer. Anything that promotes a sense of intimacy, community and connection can be healing." It has been consistently demonstrated that people who cultivate strong networks live longer, are healthier, live more fulfilling lives and maintain a positive outlook on life.

Rewarding relationships have a positive impact on our lives. Relationships are based on one of the oldest and most enduring rules of human interaction: *Do unto others as we would have others do unto us.* This maxim remains now, as it has for countless centuries, one of the cardinal rules of relationships. It is the basis of all of our moral and ethical social contracts. Protecting and respecting rewarding relationships are central ingredients in any pathfinding expedition.

## *Stay in Relationships that Help Make You a Better Person*

*One of the most important phases of maturing is that of growth from self-centering to an understanding of our relationship to others.*
(H.A. Overstreet)

*B*etty J. Eadie, author of *The Ripple Effect*, said on my radio program, Positive Living, that everything we do has a ripple effect. She discussed the need to weigh the consequences of our decisions. She said, "Everything we do in a relationship is important because it either improves the relationship or detracts from it. Positive energy creates positive connections. Negative energy causes negative ripples. We tend to copy what we receive, and give off that same energy to the people we meet."

Improving relationships means improving ourselves. A great deal of that improvement comes from treating others with respect, being sensitive to their needs and accepting them for who they are. It means establishing a partnership based on equality, loyalty and devotion, where people can maintain a mutually satisfying relationship.

David Lima M.S.W., couples counselor and author of *The Love Workbook: A Guide To Happiness In Your Personal Relationships* said, "The love workbook is all about expectations. We do have expectations about everything in life including our relationships. Generally, when our expectations are met we feel contented, happy and satisfied. The opposite is true when we don't have those expectations met and we feel dissatisfied, unhappy and discontented."

Mr. Lima defined love as "that strong positive feeling that results when your partner is meeting your expectations.

You love what your partner is doing for you and you love your partner for doing it. So it is that strong positive feeling you have that leads you to be attracted to people who are meeting your expectations."

In their book, *The New Intimacy: Discovering the Magic at the Heart of Your Differences*, Drs. Judith Sherven and James Sniechowski discuss how you can honor your partner by being curious about his or her viewpoints and choices in order to better understand and appreciate the differences.

When Judith and Jim joined my husband and me on Positive Living, we had the following insightful dialogue about accepting, learning from and eventually embracing each other's differences.

*Judith said, "When Jim and I were first together, it was clear that he loved nature. He loved clouds and trees and dogs and mountains. We lived in Los Angeles at the time and fairly often had to cross over that big mountain to get from Santa Monica to the valley. Jim would be going into great detail about the mountains, the greenery and the clouds and saying how gorgeous they were. I'd be saying, 'Would you stop it and pay attention to the freeway?' I didn't grow up appreciating nature. It just wasn't in my family to have that kind of awareness. But little by little, because Jim continued to admire the stars, the dark sky or a little flower or budding rose, I realized that he had a much fuller appreciation of life than I did. And so by osmosis, I began to be more and more aware of nature. Now, I'm often the person who says, 'Look at that cloud formation or sunrise.'"*

*"Patricia has taught me how to appreciate people in the way she relates to them and sees things that I have trouble seeing," offered my husband Antonio.*

166

*I chimed in, "I am drawn to creative, eccentric people."*

*Antonio continued, "Sometimes they don't engage in the kind of conversation I am interested in, so I lose that connection when she is still engaged in a very receptive way. As I've sat through these conversations, I have wondered what it is about this person that she likes so much. That process brings out a deeper sense of awareness."*

*Judith responded to Antonio's insight and said, "Yes, precisely, and that's why we call it 'the magic of differences.' It magically invites you to grow and expand and be able to enjoy the relationship – and all of life – more fully."*

*I said, "Antonio tried to see what I saw, which is one of the things that I really treasure in him."*

*Jim commented, "And that's called transcendence. You transcend your own world view and you practice seeing as best you can through the other person's eyes. When you do that, you generally find that what the other person is seeing is interesting, if not attractive. Then the world becomes a much larger place to live. Instead of seeing with isolated eyes, believing that 'my way is the only way,' we see the world as a much larger place to live in."*

I believe that good relationships become the basis for improving ourselves. You have a choice in how your relationships develop. By adding your own uniqueness to the soul of a relationship, you do your part to strengthen it; by withholding the authentic you, the relationship is diminished.

# *Transform Conflict Into Win-Win Relationships*

> *The influence of each human being on others in this life is a kind of immortality.*
> (John Quincy Adams)

Conflicts are doors to win-win solutions when you look for outcomes that will satisfy both parties. If you want to create resolution and a future working relationship, then you may have to compromise. But compromise doesn't mean selling out. It means finding those things you can release, so that you open a space for an outcome for the highest good of both parties. This does mean finding, acknowledging and letting go of your ego – not your principles. If you cannot reach an agreement because your values are at stake, you may have to let go of the whole situation, or take the path that will bring you the least amount of distress. Sometimes the decision to move towards win-win solutions may not reveal the true benefits for awhile – weeks, months or years. But if you feel comfort in your heart and relief in your gut, you know you've made the right decision.

An example of this concept happened to me during an interesting car repair episode:

> *I had to have my eight-year-old car repaired during one of my parent's visit. My father drove me to the dealership to pick up my car and then followed me back home. When we got home he asked to see the car repair bill. I hesitated to show him the bill because I took it as a criticism, but knew he had some words of wisdom even though I resisted hearing them.*

168

*My irritation turned to appreciation when he pointed out what he felt to be excessive charges for the labor. I called the dealer and my father spoke to the service manager. The manager justified the labor charges by referring to industry guidelines which established the repair times and rates for how long a job should take. My father told the service manager how much time he thought this job should take, which was not reflected in the bill. The service manager listened, and agreed to service my car the next time for free. I also voiced my opinion and explained to the service manager that I was not paying attention and would be a more informed consumer the next time.*

*After this incident, I said to my father, "I trusted the dealership. I thought they would take care of me."*

*"People," he said, "and that includes car dealerships, have to earn trust. Ronald Reagan once said, 'Trust, but verify.' I've found that when an organization sets guidelines, everybody is put into the same mold. You heard the service manager say that he was going by the guidelines in the book. They are only guidelines. It didn't actually take that long to fix the problem in your car. The guidelines do not favor the recipient of the service. They favor the provider of the service."*

*"I was naive, wasn't I?" I confessed. "I guess I trust people too much."*

*"It's okay to trust people. That's part of your positive living philosophy," my father replied. "Just be a little more discerning in who you trust."*

Although I still tend to give people the benefit of the doubt, I have taken my father's advice seriously. The answer, I believe, is to weigh each circumstance carefully using common sense, understand the other person's point of view and trust your own. When you put yourself in the other person's shoes, not losing sight of your own needs, you can create a win-win situation, a mutually satisfying compromise.

*Another example of creating a win-win situation happened when furniture store movers brought a new sofa to our home. They had to carry the sofa upstairs on a curved stairwell and through a narrow door. In the process, the wallpaper was nicked in the hallway. Although the nicks were small, the cost to repair them was high, because a roll of wallpaper would have to be replaced. I called the store about the incident and spoke with the owner, who was quite surprised about the cost of the damage. I was ready to return the sofa, because it appeared to be too large for the room, but that was not an option for him. I said, "My work is about positive living and I'm not hanging up this phone until we have created a win-win situation here."*

*After some discussion, the owner said that paying for the wallpaper would work for him. I wasn't sure by his tone, but when I called the store after not hearing from him, the owner's wife apologized for the delay and was very willing to send me a check, which I received a couple of days later.*

The sofa actually worked out very well and I'm happy with it. The point is that it was important for me to create a win-win situation, bringing me closure and peace.

## *Cultivate Loving Relationships*

*There is nothing greater in life than loving another and being loved in return, for loving is the ultimate of experiences.*     (Leo Buscaglia)

*W*in-win relationships lead the way to loving relationships. Of all human relationships, there are none more vital and enduring than loving relationships.

Ellen Kreidman, the author of *How to Light His Fire*, and *How to Light Her Fire,* says that people fall in love because they feel wonderful about themselves in the other person's company. A sense of oneness develops. Both members of the relationship feel valued and appreciated. A higher order of intimacy and understanding prevails. Self-esteem and personal worth are elevated. Selfishness is arrested while selflessness is given free reign. There is a special growing and nurturing dynamics that occurs through the commitment and closeness. It becomes a partnership of equals.

Loving relationships based on this kind of consideration and solidarity usually last. Enduring hardships are a joint concern. Fairness, empathy and tenderness seem to be the chief strategies loving couples use to lessen the cracks and bumps in the relationship.

Here is an example from an interview I had with Judith Sherven and James Sniechowski in discussing their latest book, *Be Loved For Who You Really Are: How the Differences between Men and Women Can Be Turned into the Source of the Very Best Romance You'll Ever Know.* Judith began by saying:

*"Early on Jim and I got into some pretty good fighting about how he tipped in restaurants. We could have fought dirty about it, in terms of calling each other names, dismissing one another, ridiculing one another, and saying things like 'You don't know what you are talking about' or 'that's a ridiculous position." What I did instead was get very curious about why it was so important for Jim not to tip at all if he felt he got poor service. That seemed unfair to me even if the person wasn't doing a good job, because they were helping and that's part of how they make their income. It wouldn't work, obviously, to just tell him to change how he tips. I had to inquire why he tipped the way he did. Then he had to inquire about why it was important to me that everybody got some kind of a tip.*

*This took us back into our background, our families of origin. We got deeper into ourselves, deeper into understanding one another and that's part of where the growth comes from. My father sold used cars all of his life and hated it. We lived in a neighborhood of professionals and I didn't want to give the impression that I came from a used car family. Jim came from factory-working Detroit, where you earned every dime. If you didn't do the job, you didn't get paid.*

*Jim summarized this point by saying, "To successfully solve a conflict you have to really want to know why the other person's position is so important to them, why it has meaning and what value it has for them. If you can explore, you begin to learn more about one another, create deeper intimacy and you can come to a mutually beneficial resolution. We've taught this process that we call Conscience Creativity to people in their teens and in their eighties. Once you learn and practice the process and your awareness grows, you can create a loving relationship in times of conflict."*

Loving relationships don't just happen. We develop and cultivate them. It requires time, patience and most of all, true respect and concern for the other person. This applies to friends and relatives as well as colleagues in the workplace. We should be caring enough to see another point of view, and understanding enough to know that working through issues is a part of love.

## *Protecting Good Relationships In Difficult Times*

*Be calm and strong and patient. Meet failure and disappointment with courage. Rise superior to the trials of life, and never give in to hopelessness or despair. In danger, in adversity, cling to your principles and ideals.* (Dr. William Osler)

*W*e all face difficult times, and the strength of our relationships is what pulls us through. Protecting good relationships in difficult times takes faith, patience and courage. I don't know a couple who has not faced difficulties. Guests on Positive Living, Drs. Les and Leslie Parrott, co-directors of the Center for Relationship Development at Seattle Pacific University and authors of *When Bad Things Happen to Good Marriages*, have this to say: "The basic premise is that every marriage starts out good. But every good marriage eventually bumps into something bad. That bad thing is always unique for each couple. There are usually four bad things that jolt good marriages to their core. They are addiction, infidelity, infertility and some kind of loss, such as the loss of a child or bankruptcy. Other predictable things are financial debt, sexual unfulfillment and communication meltdown. Things which sneak up on good marriages include business demands, irritability, boredom and drifting apart."

On what helps people get through the bad times, the Parrotts said, "In a single sentence it's the capacity to adjust to things beyond their control. Time and time again we have found that they had the ability to find an upbeat attitude in spite of their circumstances. We also know from research that those couples that share those deeper values in common make life in marriage much easier."

The Parrotts outlined five major tools for getting through rough times. They are: taking ownership without blaming each other; finding hope in the midst of difficulties; having empathy for the other person's perspective; forgiveness; and commitment to the relationship.

Another relationship expert on the program, Dr. Margaret Paul, nationally-acclaimed author, facilitator, seminar leader and co-author of *Do I Have to Give Up Me to Be Loved By You?* discussed how couples can work through difficulties in ways that create more love and intimacy.

The premise of her book is there are only two intentions possible in any given moment – the intent to learn and the intent to protect. "In the intention to protect we do not take responsibility for our feelings. We want to avoid our feelings at all costs through some form of controlling behavior. In the intention to learn, we want to learn about and take full responsibility for all of our feelings including pain and joy as well as our beliefs and behavior that may be causing our difficult feelings."

To stay open and loving in a relationship when there is conflict, she said, "This requires a personal decision of what is really important to the person in a broader and spiritual sense. The question to answer is whether we are here to get love or to evolve in becoming loving human beings. The decision to get love will always lead to protective and controlling behavior. When our deeper intention is to evolve into loving human beings, to manifest our dreams, and to really express ourselves in the most loving way possible, our behavior will naturally follow from that."

On how to discuss conflict with the other person she said, "I encourage people to let the other person know you don't like their behavior and tell them what you plan to do to take care of yourself in the face of their unloving behavior. Tell them what your limits are."

When you have clear expectations and know your limits, it's easier to see the big picture without getting bogged down in details that are really not important in the large scheme of things. This requires discipline, because it is so easy to get caught up in having our needs met on a daily basis. Being aware, loving, grateful and respectful for the gifts that you and the other person give each other will bring you more.

# *The Specialness of Father/Daughter Relationships*

*Because of the life I've lived, I know there is only one way I can live the life I have left–as a spiritual odyssey driven by an unbreakable promise, a solemn oath, a sacred vow to my father, to carry (his) torch, to illuminate the spirit in every song I sing and in every place I go.* (Patti LaBelle)

*E*ver since I was a little girl, I felt a special closeness to my father. Call it telepathy or some type of psychic connection. We've always understood each other. I have disagreed with some of my father's observations and interpretations of the vicissitudes of life through the years, and he with mine. My father and I took different paths. We are of different generations. He is the first generation son of immigrants and I am a second generation babyboomer. He is strongly imbedded in Hebrew teachings and in Jewish literature. I have turned to the spiritual teachings of several religions and believe strongly in the power of our own inner guidance.

Now I'm in my middle years and my dad in his 80's. I remember the wisdom my father has offered me through his years in medicine, his religious teachings and his own life experiences. As a guest on Positive Living for Father's Day, he pointed out to me that the *Bible* says, 'Thou shalt teach it diligently unto thy children' which means to teach them how to live as decent human beings." And teach me he did. I am still enjoying the benefits of his insights and wisdom.

*I remember when I was just small, probably three or four, I was an overly active child. I vividly remem-*

176

*ber banging my head against the seat in the car as my father drove. Today, I regain that same rhythm from dancing and fast walking on the beach or treadmill, and this movement has become a requirement for my body.*

*That rhythmic movement from banging my head in the car proved to be a "sleep-saver" in my early childhood because it was difficult for me to go to sleep. My father would drive me around the block a couple of times in the car until the motion of the car would rock me to sleep. I shared that story on Father's Day in June of 2000 during one of my program segments. My father was on the show and it remains one of my most endearing media moments. During the show, I asked my father if he remembered driving me around the neighborhood.*

*"I often think about those short trips," he said. "As a matter of fact, I used to cradle you in my arms as I drove. I would probably have gotten arrested by the child safety police for driving like that today. I used to drive you around to settle you down so you'd go to sleep."*

*When I look back on those early years, I remember how fortunate I was to be able to spend the time I could with you. I had just gotten out of the military service. I practiced dentistry in a little town called Wethersfield, Connecticut. I set up an office in our home. Of course, business wasn't as brisk then as it is today. You were my first born. I wasn't going to miss those early years. I always did my part in raising you, playing with you and nurturing you."*

*He then reflected on rearing children today, and said: "Children are left to their own devices and a lot of them have never experienced the closeness of family. They feel abandoned and displaced. This is part of*

177

*the problem. Families have got to stick together and work together. They need to show each other how much they love one another."*

Shortly after the show, my father shared a story from his childhood with me:

> *I had earned nine dollars one morning and thought I'd celebrate my success by going to a movie. Movies only cost twenty-five cents back then. The nine dollars would probably be the equivalent of a couple of hundred dollars today. I enjoyed the movie, but when I got home, I realized I had lost my wallet. I ran back to the movie theater, but my wallet was gone.*
>
> *I was heartbroken. Times were tough and my mother needed the money. The next day the local druggist called and told me someone had found my wallet. Unfortunately, when I retrieved it, the money was gone. I felt cheated a second time.*
>
> *To this day, I remember my mother's attempts to console me. She said 'Zunela (diminutive Yiddish expression for son) don't be sad. As much as we need the money, perhaps the person who took it needs it more than we do.'*
>
> *I have often thought about the "mitzvahs" (Hebrew word for kind deed or considerate act) my mother gave me on that occasion and on many occasions to follow. Her words have stayed with me all of these years.*

Family stories like these are dear to me. They are wonderful memories. My pathfinding has taken me back to my childhood and given me the perspective I need to appreciate my adulthood. My journey has triggered memories and lessons which I shall always cherish. My desire to fully understand my connection with my father has gone beyond the father/daughter relationship. It has been altered somewhat by the realization that I am a married professional woman who has taken on the considerable project of writing her second book. From this perspective, I have gained a clearer view of the man who is my father. Through the trials and triumphs of parenthood, he tried to prepare me for the challenges he knew the world would lay at my feet.

My best friend from childhood, Ellen Garber Rosow, has a similar story of her own. Her father was a nurturer and catalyst. Ellen remembers fondly:

*"What my father gave me was a sense of security and stability. He was there at every turn. I loved being with him. He wanted me in his life. He enjoyed my company and was proud of me. He took me to the bank with him all the time and on errands with him. Whenever I asked him, he would take me somewhere. There was rarely hesitation.*

*"That continued unto my adult life. When I had young children and needed him to babysit, he was there. Whether it was to take my children to dance lessons or basketball practices, or stay several days with them while my husband and I travelled, I always felt confident leaving my children in my father and mother's care.*

*"Later in life the tables were turned and he needed help because of poor health," Ellen continued. In his last few months I remained by his side, going every day to the hospital. I took off the last two weeks*

*of his life and slept by his side. I told him how much I loved him. I hope I eased him toward his next passage.*

*"I have fond memories of my father. He taught me diplomacy and tact, generosity and thankfulness. He was adamant about showing people dignity and respect. I will always miss him. You are so lucky that your father is still living."*

I certainly agree with Ellen. I thank God every day that both of my parents are alive. I feel blessed to be able to visit them and to vacation with them.

As an adult child, I encourage you to develop a deeper relationship with your parents. Learn about them as individuals, as imperfect human beings living in an imperfect world. Discover why they made the decisions they did and how those attitudes and values affected their lives and yours. Settle your differences. Celebrate your connection. Honor each other's individuality. Deepen your trust and appreciation for each other. Find the specialness – it's there!

# *Give and Accept Acts of Loving Kindness*

*I shall pass through this world but once. If, therefore, there be any kindness I can show, or any good things I can do, let me do it now.*

(William Penn)

*P*erforming and accepting acts of love and kindness in a positive manner can diminish or even eliminate hate and prejudice. Civilized society has not always faced this issue. One of the most shining examples of a *tsaddick* (Yiddish word for a righteous person), is Jackie Waldman, who after being diagnosed with multiple sclerosis, found purpose in working with the Dallas Memorial Center of Holocaust Studies. I introduced her in Chapter 3 as a shining example of a person who transforms obstacles into opportunities. Jackie is the author of *The Courage to Give: Inspiring stories of People Who Triumphed Over Tragedy to Make a Difference in the World,* and *Teens With Courage to Give: Young People Who Triumphed Over Tragedy to Make a Difference in the World.* She launched the Dallas Random Acts of Kindness™ Movement and was chosen by CNN as one of their millennium heroes.

Jackie Waldman's new book, *America, September 11th – The Courage to Give,* was recently published. The book contains stories of 37 people, from Ground Zero to firefighters to Pentagon heroes, all across the country. Ten of the stories are original; the other 27 are reprints from newspapers who have waived the copyright fees. All monies from the book will go to help victims of the September 11th tragedy.

Jackie Waldman's message is, "When you have that courage to give and to step out of your own story to reach out into the lives of family, friends and strangers, then whence you go back to your own story, you gain a new perspective. When you have had something happen to you, and you have the courage to give, you see your own worthiness and your self-esteem immediately come back. When you help someone else and touch or change someone's life and you are so grateful that you are able to use your own unique gift doing what you love and sharing it, that's when miracles happen."

Linda Riley, a recent guest on Positive Living, is the author of *The Call to Love: Unleashing the Power to Love God and Others in Your Everyday Life.* She told a personal story from her own life that illustrates the power of kindness, "We left a tip for a waitress a couple of months ago and wrote a note which said, 'God is thinking about you today.' When we went back to that restaurant, the waitress came running up to us and asked if we were the ones who left the note along with the generous tip. She pulled out the small book where she kept her credit card receipts and showed us our note. She told us she looks at the note everyday and shows it to the other waitresses and waiters. That small act of kindness brought her a lot of comfort."

There are more examples of known and unknown acts of love and kindness. My father told me this story:

*In the mid-30's when I was in college, jobs were hard to find. One summer I was lucky to get a Saturday morning job from 6:00 a.m. to noon unloading banana boats in Boston. My first assignment involved carrying what they called a stalk of bananas from the hold of the ship up vertical steps to the processing area offshore.*

> *The stalks were trimmed into hands for the bananas to be packaged for shipping. The weight of each stalk varied from forty to eighty pounds. They hung from the ceiling of the ship's hold in rows. Each of us would wear a rubber shoulder apron and stand beneath the next stalk. The man standing there would cut the string holding the stalk and it would drop onto your shoulder. Then burdened with the heavy stalk, you'd walk up the stairs to the processing areas.*
>
> *It was backbreaking work. But I'll never forget the time it was my luck, or misfortune, to stand under an oversized stalk. I had difficulty carrying that load up the steps. I didn't think I would make it. Suddenly, out of nowhere, a hand took me by the seat of my pants and pushed me up the ladder until I could gain my balance and carry the load to the processing room. When I turned around to see who had given me that wonderful helpful hand, I looked directly into the face of a huge African-American man. At the time he had pushed me up the ladder, he was carrying his own load. I'll never forget the kind look on his face. It taught me to appreciate kindness wherever and from whomever I find it.*

Every time you receive an act of kindness, it is an act that has been given to you by someone. Another example is the story of Charles Graham who gave one of his kidneys to Clem Williams.

> *On the radio, Charles mentioned a visit to his friend, Joey Griffin, in the hospital. He was told that Joey needed a kidney to stay alive. Charles unhesitat-*

*ingly offered one of his own. I asked Charles why he was willing to do this and he responded, "I love helping people if I can, and Joey is a friend of mine." As it turned out, Charles' kidney was not a match for Joey, but Joey fortunately did get a kidney from another source.*

*The story took on a twist when Joey told Charles about Clem Williams, who also needed a kidney. Clem lived in the same coastal North Carolina town as Joey and his friend Charles. Charles again offered his kidney. After receiving word that his sister's kidney was not a match, Clem was delighted to find that Charles's kidney was a perfect match.*

*I asked Charles about the process of giving his kidney. He said, "It's quite a process. I had to undergo a series of tests including blood panels, an IVP, ultrasound and twenty-four hour urine analysis among other procedures. But I would do it again. I've gotten great satisfaction out of knowing I was able to help Clem live. He is able to do things now that he was unable to do at one time. It makes me feel good knowing I was able to help him."*

*On what the kidney donation meant to Clem, who was a science teacher, coach of national champions and administrator for many years, he said, "What Charles did for me was give me a second chance at life. At that point in my life, being a diabetic and having long-term kidney failure, I was just about ready to give up. Charles' generosity renewed my faith. It has made me acutely aware of other people's needs. One of the reasons I returned to teaching and tutoring is to help students who really need a pat on the back and encouragement. I believe that if you work hard enough, you can overcome the odds. If you need some help, don't be afraid to ask for it and don't give up.*

*There are plenty of people out there who will give you a helping hand."*

*Since that time, Clem went on to have an additional surgery – he had a pancreatic transplant as well. Today however, blood tests as well as his kidney function are normal.*

*"I don't have be told by somebody that prayer works. I know it works. In addition, attitude is a must. I am older, wiser and I listen more acutely. I am more aware of myself," Clem said. Clem walks ten miles a day on the cross trainer at the gym and receives a glowing bill of health from his doctors. In his 60's, he says he has more energy than he did in his 40's. He sees Charles weekly and together the pair volunteer time to Carolina Donor Services. Clem also tutors at-risk youth in the area. "I love my life. I love my wife and children. I didn't think I'd see my son and daughter get married," said Clem. But thanks to the life saving surgeries and his own positive attitude and diligence, Clem has a new lease on life.*

In the stories I've heard like these, there is a common thread; they are all shining moments. You will find, as you look back on your own life that moments such as these stand out, they are eternal tributes to the basic goodness and kindness of the human spirit.

There is a Hebrew proverb which says, "Kindness is the beginning and end of the law." It is the little, thoughtful acts of kindness that make a big difference in people's lives – both for the giver and the receiver. I agree with Douglas Bloch who said, "No act of kindness, however small, is ever wasted."

Loving kindness and generosity have no boundaries. One of the 613 commandments in Judaism obliges you to help people in trouble even if they are your enemies. My father tells a wonderful story about kindness:

> *Two mule drivers were traveling near each other when the donkey of one of them fell over under the burden. The driver, who owned the poor mules, started to unload the animal. It was a very difficult task. The second driver, who hated the first driver, saw the predicament he was in. Surprisingly he helped him unload. He helped his enemy even though his enemy was in trouble. This is called a "mitzvah" a kind deed. Because of that act of kindness the two became friends.*

I believe acts of kindness result in acts of kindness. I'm going to share another one of my father's stories because it epitomizes the very nature of kindness and loyalty:

> *Once there was a kind, gentle and charitable man, who never turned a needy person away. He held an esteemed position in his community. Through a series of unforeseen circumstances, he lost his successful business, his home and all his possessions. He moved to another town but found himself reduced to begging and doing menial tasks to exist.*
>
> *One day, a passerby said to him, "Why don't you ask the rich miser, Jake, for some work? He always needs help, and will surely take advantage of your need. But at least you will not have to beg to live. Let me warn you though, he is abusive, cruel and demanding. Everybody hates him and nobody will work for him."*

186

> *The poor man was in such need that he asked the miser for a job. He was offered the lowly task of personal servant. The master, true to his nature, was grouchy, demanding, insulting and at times impossible. For many years, the poor man ignored the horrible actions exhibited by his master. He remained a faithful servant and treated his master with respect.*
>
> *The townspeople would take the poor servant aside and criticize his loyalty to a crusty, aggravating master.*
>
> *However, the personal servant would always say, "This is the only way I know how to treat others."*
>
> *There came a day when the master fell gravely ill. The doctors told him that he was on his death bed, he called for his faithful servant and said to him, "You have been a faithful loving servant to me for many years. You have endured my insults and aggravating taunts and my very bad behavior. I acted this way because I felt that everybody in town was scheming to part me from my riches. But by your behavior I had confidence that you were a decent and honest person. Before I die, to make amends with you and God, I am leaving my entire fortune to you. And the man died shortly thereafter.*

This story told by my father is adapted from Rabbinic literature. "The moral of the story," my father says, "is that kindness and love may be difficult to exhibit in circumstances which are not favorable, but never underestimate the power of kindness even under the most difficult circumstances."

I have found that treating people with kindness and respect accelerates pathfinding. The old axiom I mentioned earlier in this chapter, "What goes around comes around," really is true. Acts of loving kindness disintegrate barriers, eliminate obstacles and straighten the detours in life. Words of kindness are words of wellness, and acts of kindness are acts of healing. I believe you will not find your path unless you find kindness first. And if you do not find kindness, none of the paths you find will be kind to you. So take kinder, gentler steps on your way to selfhood.

## *Relationships Foster Human Connectedness and Understanding*

*Two consciousnesses, each dedicated to personal evolution, can provide an extraordinary stimulus and challenge to the other...(their relationship) becomes the pathway...to the higher reaches of human growth.*

(Nathaniel Branden)

*K*eeping relationships vibrant and healthy is like keeping our body vibrant and healthy. It takes exercise and conscious choice making. It means choosing your words wisely and opening your heart as well as your mind to listen and understand. It also means having the belief that you want peace, harmony and win-win relationships in your life. This requires a lot more than you may realize. It means asking yourself the question, 'Will the action I am about to take bring me peace of mind?' Peace of mind translates into good health because so much of our disease is caused by stress and burnout.

Beyond our intimate relationships, we can extend the principles discussed here to all of our relationships, from the cashier in the grocery store, the waiter in the restaurant, the acquaintance we see on the street, to our colleagues, as this story told by my father illustrates:

> *A group of archaeologists were having lunch together at a convention. During the course of conversation, one of the lesser known members took a coin out of his pocket, and with extremely great pride, fervor and glee, announced that this coin was extremely rare, and was the only one like it in the world. He passed it around the table for all his colleagues to examine.*
>
> *With the luncheon coming to a close, the owner of the coin asked for its return. It could not be found. Everybody searched high and low, but it was not to be found. After several excruciating minutes of searching, one of the archaeologists suddenly announced, 'Here it is!'*
>
> *With grateful relief, the owner retrieved the coin, and thanked his colleague. Suddenly, one of the waiters entered the room and, holding up a coin, announced, 'Who does this belong to?' It was another coin exactly like the other one.*

*Needless to say, this created an uproar among the members. They wondered how this could be. And then came the explanation; one of the most famous and well known archaeologists admitted that the first coin belonged to him. It had it been recently found in one of his expeditions. He explained that he did not wish to hurt the pride of his younger colleague, who had displayed such exuberance in the belief that he was the sole possessor of such a rare find.*

This kind of consideration, which is as rare as the coin itself, reminds us of our great possibilities as humankind to be humane and kind to each other. This next story, told during my program by Jill Lawrence, national award-winning journalist and host of "Jill & Friends," really shows us the profound effect even strangers can have in our lives, if only for a few seconds.

*I learned a great lesson from Ranelle Wallace, who wrote The Burning Within. Her story is a long and staggering one. She was in a horrific plane crash and suffered burns over all her body. She was critically wounded, yet managed to walk 5 miles down a mountain in order to save her life. Once they finally got an ambulance, she lapsed and clinically died, experiencing a near death experience.*

*It was an incredible experience. I've heard many near death experiences on my program, but what I heard from her really impacted my life and, I hope, the lives of others. As she was reviewing her life and looking at every single thought and every single day she'd been in, she saw a time when she was walking down the street. A woman was walking towards her on a sidewalk who was an utter stranger. Ranelle smiled at the stranger and they passed. The only contact they had was that Ranelle smiled at her.*

*In her near death experience, she got to see the ramifications of that smile. It turns out that woman was on her way home to commit suicide, and because Ranelle smiled at her, it gave her enough hope to keep going. In a near death experience, you get to see what impact your actions had on others. In this case, a simple smile really saved another woman's life.*

Whether or not you believe in the validity of near death experiences, the effect of a smile, a thank you, a cheerful voice on the phone, can make the difference in your day and in the next action you take toward another person. Kindness and radiating love is felt by others because we transmit energy by our presence. Have you ever noticed how a group of people without the regulars in attendance, changes the energy and exchanges within the group? We all have such a profound impact on each other, often much more than we realize.

This was exemplified during the September 11 terrorist attack on our country. Along with the tragedy came a great uprising of hope, connectedness and love. I interviewed Michael Feldschuh, founder of *The September 11 Photo Project*, a picture book highlighting the open forum for display of photographs in response to the terrorist attacks. Michael has, with the help of many people, compiled a book of about 200 pages. The photos, in both black and white and color, were taken through the eyes of the participants who witnessed the event.

On how his own life has changed since September 11, Michael said, "My life has become a lot richer. It's been an opportunity for me to work with a lot of wonderful people and to make a difference." He added, "Never underestimate the ability of people to come together to give to one another. Sometimes the very best in people comes out in situations like this."

Michael closed the interview with eloquent words of hope about the positive things that we can take from the tragedy of September 11. He said, "It's the value of being connected to others, and the way to do this is to bear witness to what they have gone through. It's the principle of putting yourself in the place of another, of seeing and witnessing where they are. That is fostering human connectedness and understanding and I think that we all have a strong desire and need to be connected to one another. That sounds easy but it's actually incredibly difficult. We have to take the time to read, think, understand and experience the perspective of others. That will enrich ourselves and others. I think that the positive thing that can come out of this is that we all have a much deeper understanding of violence, its impact on our society and the need for peace."

Michael is describing the effects kindness has on a society, and perhaps even the world. Kindness is contagious. Loving acts of kindness begin in little ways, in moments of sensitivity and humility. I believe true kindness and generosity require more of us than a kindly impulse. Kind-heartedness is the capacity to see people in all of their complexity, perplexity and needs – and to know how to share ourselves effectively and lovingly with them.

Generosity and kindness do not have to be magnanimous acts. They can be simple, almost noticeable acts of goodness. I love the way Emily Dickinson described it. "They might need a little, but they might need much," she said, "I'll let my head be just in sight; a smile as small as mine might be precisely their necessity." Kindness is the poetry of the heart, the music of the soul. Kind words and loving deeds come from a goodness that turns everything positive. Kindness is so inexpensive, yet so priceless. It comes from a loving heart, and like love, it can't be forced, coaxed or teased out. It comes from deep within us at a soul level, unasked and unsought.

## *Forgive Others and Make Peace With the Past*

*"What's gone and past help, should be past grief. Things without remedy, should be without regard; what is done is done."*

(William Shakespeare)

*B*eing kind and forgiving is part of making peace with our past. It also means accepting who we are, what we are, and what has happened to us. We are surrounded by the past in pictures, our mistakes, our bodies as we age, the possessions we have that hold memories. I feel that one of the keys to happiness is to appreciate and forgive the people who have been part of our journey.

When I asked Jill Lawrence her advice to listeners from the thousands of inspirational and spiritual authors, she said, "Perhaps the most important thing is to forgive yourself and others. Right next to that is to focus on love, to bathe yourself in love and to bathe everyone you're around in love. It can't be over emphasized to be really aware and conscious because it is truly real that your thoughts and your words create absolute matter in your life."

Dr. Harold H. Bloomfield, nationally-renowned psychiatrist, multiple New York Times bestselling author, and author of *Making Peace with your Past: The Six Essential Steps to Enjoying a Great Future*, believes we must recognize, reframe and release the emotional chains of the past, see the present as a gift and view the future filled with possibilities. Dr. Bloomfield said on my program, "People realize they can't find inner peace and create a truly satisfying life unless they heal emotional wounds of the past. What they may not realize is that they could also be saving their lives. When you forgive your past, you can turn fully towards the future."

Dr. Bloomfield encouraged listeners to experience the source of deep peace within by releasing emotional chains of the past. He explained that ways to access this peaceful state are learning new habits of self-care, understanding the lessons and gifts from traumatic experiences in your life, having an attitude of gratitude, seeking sources of wisdom and information, being in the present moment and spending time meditating, walking, breathing and praying as a couple.

Dr. Bloomfield discussed the messages and patterns that we learned about love and sex and how we translate them into our current relationships. He said, "It's important to really look at how you were loved, the problems you had with a difficult parent, and who the ghosts are that haunt you."

One of the key messages from guests on my program is to not dwell on the past or to allow past experiences to weigh us down. This has been a challenge and personal lesson for me. I think it's productive to look back and learn from our past defeats only in order to make future course corrections.

This is a story that deals with releasing the ghosts of the past. It is told by a very sensitive and renowned plastic surgeon, Dr. Robert Goldwyn, who wrote the pioneering book

194

*The Patient and The Plastic Surgeon* over thirty years ago. This story is an excerpt from my husband Antonio's radio program, "Plastic Surgery Today," that received the 2001 Circle of Excellence Media Award from the American Society of Plastic Surgeons. What is most exciting about receiving the award for this particular program is that it focuses on the doctor-patient relationship, not on the latest procedure. Dr Goldwyn shared:

> *I had a patient who saw me for breast reconstruction before she had a mastectomy. She did not want to have a mastectomy. In my conversation with her, and I spent two or three hours total over two consultations, I found out that she had survived a concentration camp in Nazi Germany. She did not want to have surgery because she did not want to be deformed. I remember very clearly that she was my last patient, she was from another state and it was a Friday afternoon. I said to her, 'Mrs. So and So, I want you to know that Hitler would be very, very happy to know that he couldn't eliminate you during the war, but you're eliminating yourself.' I took a chance with her because that is not something that you would ordinarily say. And when she left the office, I said to myself, 'I really did it this time.' On Monday she called the office and said, 'I'm going to have that surgery.' She's been well now for twenty years. This wouldn't have happened if the doctor said, 'Well, if you don't want the surgery, fine. Next patient please.' But if you listen, you know that there had to be a reason she acted this way before she had the surgery."*

Obviously these exact words would not work with every patient. The point is recognizing the amazing power of listening to each individual, and responding appropriately. Because Dr. Goldwyn took the extra time to listen and "put himself on the line" to get to the root cause of the patient's fear of surgery, he was able to help this patient release the past, which in this case most likely meant saving her life.

As guest Michael Lewis, Ph.D., Director of the Institute for the Study of Child Development at Robert Wood Johnson Medical School, and author of *Altering Fate: Why the Past Does Not Predict the Future*, put so aptly in his book, "Our early experiences do not seal our fate, nor do they determine who we are or limit what we can do." According to Dr. Lewis, we can change our circumstances by acts of will and desire.

The most obvious thing about the past is to remember that whatever happened in the past is history. It's part of our past, our unrecoverable experience. Any time we find ourselves quarreling or complaining about what should have been or what we could have done, we would be much better off focusing on what we can do now. Since we can only live in the present, it is preposterous and self-negating to dwell fruitlessly on the past. This is a principle that I am still working on. I still catch myself saying, "I should have done that" or "I could have done this." That kind of thinking helps us make course corrections for the future, but in most cases, post-mortems accomplish nothing.

Making peace with the past means recognizing that our parents did the best they could with what they had. Our relatives did what they knew how to do. Our brothers and sisters expressed themselves as best they could. Whatever disappointments and unfortunate events that might have happened to us happened for a reason. The important lesson is to move on. The past doesn't have to haunt us forever, unless we want it to.

Learn from the past and refuse to allow past events to impede your future. Have the courage to mend family fences. Forgive yourself, and forgive others, for mistakes and misunderstandings. Work tirelessly to keep the past in its place. Don't allow self-defeating thoughts, attitudes and behaviors to creep into the present. Work hard at changing what you can to improve family relationships. Accept what you can't control or change. I've learned along my journey that when you've made peace with yourself, you've made peace with the past.

I agree with my dear friend and certified professional coach Bobbi Gemma, who says, "We need to define the essence of what we really want...in relationships...The joy of (relationships) is about appreciation. It's appreciating our lives, the world we live in...and each other."

## *Positive Pollination*

*List:*
- ❖ The childhood experiences that brought you the most joy.
- ❖ Special moments with loved ones, family, friends, co-workers and colleagues.
- ❖ The relationships in your life that are based on equality, loyalty and respect.
- ❖ People you can depend on to give you honest feedback.
- ❖ Your definition of love.
- ❖ Your definition of friendship.

*Reflect on:*
- ❖ Ways you have lovingly resolved or can resolve conflicts in your relationship.
- ❖ Ways you have forgiven or can forgive relationships that have brought you pain.
- ❖ Ways you show your appreciation to those special people in both your personal and professional lives.
- ❖ Ways you can keep important relationships healthy and vibrant.

CHAPTER SEVEN

# Believe in Miracles

*There are only two ways to live your life.*
*One is as though nothing is a miracle. The*
*other is as though everything is a miracle.*
(Albert Einstein)

*I* believe in miracles. I also believe we can create them by our thoughts. We've all experienced those "coincidences" when someone we have just been thinking of calls us or we bump into the person we really needed to talk to, or we find the right thing at exactly the right time, or we miss a mishap by seconds. If you really want to experience a miracle, ask for it, pray for it and truly believe you will receive it. You won't have to work at it because *something* greater than you is at work. I define that *something* as God.

Scriptures are full of miraculous events, myths and legends. In all of the world's religions miracles function as a sign and a wondrous event. As wonders they incite awe, as signs they signify the present of a divine power who was intensely interested in human affairs. Religious miracles usually involve weeping statues and paintings, works of art which seem to move on their own, images of saints which appear and disappear. There are miraculous encounters of people being saved by an unknown being or healed by someone with extraordinary extrasensory abilities. Some people see crosses of light or other religious materializations like white light, silhouettes of Christ or the Virgin Mary.

These highly inspirational religious phenomena occur worldwide to unrelated people or groups who witness the miracle. Although most of the miracles involve subjective experiences, many are substantiated with physical, objective proof. Western science has not endorsed the miraculous as scientific fact. However, there are lines of thought in contemporary psychology, physics, neurophysiology and biology that suggest a strong connection between miraculous phenomena and human transpersonal growth.

In a discussion about miracles with my father, he said:

*"Jewish rabbis believe God works through angels. In Rabbinic lore, there is a group of unknown characters in the world who are called 'lamed-vovnicks.' Lamed denotes the number 30 in Hebrew. Vov denotes the Hebrew number 6. The suffix 'nicks' is an idiom which means 'pertaining to people.' This means that in the entire world there are 36 anonymous people who are God's closest angels roaming the world. Their individual deeds affect all of humanity. Possible 'lamed-vovnicks' are such individuals as Mother Teresa, Albert Schweitzer or Rabbi Meier Kagan, who in human form, could have been one of God's 36 closest and most trusted angels. Only the degree of kindness, humaneness and love indicates the possibility of that person being one of the 36."*

The 'lamed-vovnicks' my father mentioned are real. Talmudic literature (Rabbinic Judaism lore) contains a number of documented miracle stories about a few extraordinary sages. Historical sources from many cultures talk about these beings. They are referred to as enlightened ones, holy ones, or highly evolved beings. Their express purpose is to help humanity resolve crises on a global, as well as personal level. For those of you who want to do more reading on the subject, there are hundreds of books available. Some of the most recent are: *We Believe in Miracles* by Juliet O'Neill, *The Book of Miracles* by K. L. Woodard, *Masters Among Us* by T. Curley, *Crosses of Light and Other Miracles* by T. Gros and P. S. Koberne, and *Extraordinary Times, Extraordinary Beings* by W. Peterson.

I asked my father if he had ever met a "lamed-vovnick" and he said, "I don't know. I have met many people who have been good and kind to me as well as others. But even amongst these so-called angels, there are differing degrees of intensity of kindness and goodness. To me, one of the great mysteries of life is that we really don't know who the *lamed-vovnicks* or who any angels are for that matter. The only possible way they can be determined is by the degree of kindness, humaneness and love which they exude. You may consider a person is an angel if he or she acts in a kindly manner. Just by saying thank you, writing a note of appreciation, or being positive in a negative situation may be fulfilling an angelic mission stimulated by an unknown power."

I asked my father if this unknown power is God, he said, "How else can you explain it? When you put miracles into perspective, this is not about religion. Kindness is kindness no matter who performs it. I have come to believe that ordinary human beings, like their *lamed-vovnick* counterparts, can display extraordinary kindness, love and grace."

On some level, God is doing extraordinary things through human beings. "Speculation about (miracles) is hardly any different," says Dr. Scott Peck, author of the bestseller *The Road Less Traveled* and many other books, "from speculation about God having at His command armies and choirs of archangels, angels, seraphims and cherubims to assist Him in the task of ordering the universe...The mind, which sometimes presumes to believe there is no such thing as a miracle, is itself a miracle."

## *Find the Miraculous in the Ordinary*

*Miracles occur naturally as expressions of love. The real miracle is the love that inspires them. In this sense everything that comes from love is a miracle.* (Marianne Williamson)

*O*ne must establish what constitutes a miracle," my father says. "And it's not an easy task. What is perceived as a miracle by some, is not considered a miracle by others." He points out that, in Rabbinic lore, by the 18th century Jewish mysticism described prominent rabbis as "tzaddikim" (righteous ones), thereby imparting exceptional holiness to them and viewing them as messengers of God. In parts of Israel today, there are "rebbes" who are regarded as possessing unusual powers and mystical abilities. He

202

shares the Yisroel Meir Kagan story, which explains how people view the nature of miracles differently:

> *Rabbi Yisroel Meir Kagan was born and raised in Radin Poland. He had a grocery store, and because of his reputation and fame people would flock to his store, causing his competitor to do badly. The rabbi soon realized that he was hurting the other grocer, who was not Jewish. So, he closed his store because he felt that it was not fair for him to capitalize on his fame to do harm to another person. He was considerate of all people regardless of their religious beliefs. He wrote several books, one of which was entitled 'The Evil Tongue,' which characterizes the tongue as man's worst weapon. A gun or knife may kill once but words from the tongue will kill over and over again. I learned all this when my oldest grandson was named after this man and I read the story of his life.*
>
> *When Rabbi Kagan died, he was buried in the Jewish cemetery in the town of Radin, Poland. During World War II, the town of Radin was in the middle of the war zone between the Germans and the Russians. The town was repeatedly overrun, first by the Germans, then by the Russians. Yet, the town was never destroyed or damaged in a significant way. After the war, his family wanted to have the rabbi reburied in Israel. However, the non-Jewish population objected to the removal of his body, and blocked the reburial because they felt that Rabbi Kagan was a saintly man who had spent his life caring for people regardless of their*

*religious beliefs. The people of Radin perceived that they had escaped death and destruction during the war because of the saintliness of this one man. Was it a miracle? They certainly thought so.*

Both my father and I agree that it was God's doing. On my radio program, I have been privy to similar stories which reinforce my belief in the power of miracles.

I talked about the courage of Bill Irwin in Chapter 3. Bill is the author of *Blind Courage*, and with his dog Orient, became the first blind person to thru-hike the 2,100 mile Appalachian Trail. The thru-hike took Mr. Erwin 8 1/2-months or 258 days. The inspiration to hike the trail was a miracle in itself, which he describes:

*"The journey was a mandate, which was proven to me before I even got started. That's why I became willing to do it. You have to udnerstand where I was coming from. Due to my life of alcoholism, alcohol-induced hepatitis and ultimately losing my sight at age 28, I was dealing with some pretty emotional life issues. I remember doing a healing session with my son one weekend on the Blue Ridge Parkway in Virginia. I became overwhelmed with the beautiful world God gave us to enjoy, and made Him a promise that 'if there is anything I can do to show You how grateful I am for what you've done for me and my son this weekend, let me know what it is and I'll do it.' Then I forgot all about that conversation.*

*You'd better be very careful about what you say to God, because He doesn't forget! All of a sudden, without any interest on my part, I started receiving information about the Appalachian Trail. I didn't even know where the Trail was, let alone the extent of it. I'd never been backpacking in my life, except for one small weekend camping trip when I was a Boy Scout. So I asked myself why I was receiving eight separate pieces of information about different aspects of the Appalachian Trail?*

*"Most of the people who sent me the information did not know each other, so the chances of this being a conspiracy were zero. I decided to call each person, some of whom I hadn't heard from in over 30 years. When I called, I asked them this question: 'Why did you send me that information?' I got exactly the same answer from all eight people – 'I felt lead to do it.' I responded, 'Is that it? Can you give me more detail?' They would say, 'No, I just had this overpowering feeling that I was supposed to send this information to you.'*

*"One of the people who sent me information was my son, who mailed an application to a school that taught how to do the Appalachian Trail in a week. I asked him where he got it. He said he picked it up at a camping store in Chapel Hill. I asked, 'Well why'd you send it to me?' He responded, 'I just had this feeling.' I had never mentioned anything about the Appalachian Trail to him or anyone else. I never even thought about it.*

*"Most of the people who sent me material weren't spiritual, let alone religious, but I know that the inspiration was divine. It was definitely a spiritual journey that without God's help would have been absolutely impossible. As more time passes, I'm more convinced of that. In fact, there are hundreds of people now that are blind who have tried doing what I did and no one's succeeded."*

Dr. Lou Tartaglia, psychiatrist and frequent co-host on my radio program, is the narrator of the audio program *Thirsting for God: Spiritual Lessons of Mother Teresa* by Nightingale-Conant. Dr. Tartaglia is the co-author with Father Angelo Scolozzi who worked with Mother for more than two decades.

Lou introduced me to Father Angelo who worked with Mother Teresa in India. In my conversation with Father Angelo, he said:

*"For 21 years I served with Mother Teresa. Prior to that, I was a Benedictine monk. I will never forget how I felt when I first met her. It was a magic moment for me.*

*"When I saw and felt her goodness, I pictured in my mind Mary, the mother of Jesus. But her clothing was typical of India. Mother Teresa was wearing a white sari with a blue border. She wore no shoes like many of the people of India with whom she worked. Once a ray of light came through the window and seemed to brighten her figure which reinforced by feeling that she was Mary incarnate. She was very single hearted. She was a woman of purpose. Whatever limitations she possessed, she turned into strengths. One of her famous sayings, 'Let's do small things with great love.'*

*"It seemed that all of her accomplishments were miraculous. I remember an incident where a child in Calcutta desperately needed a particular medicine that was not available in India. It only came from England. Mother Teresa asked the British airlines to have the pilot bring the medicine to her. Just before the airplane took off, the pharmacy sent over a surplus of medicines and the vital medication was placed on top of the basket of medicine. I could only feel that God*

*had great love for that dying child in Calcutta. When Mother Teresa learned what had happened she exclaimed, 'that's the great miracle.' Mother Teresa taught us never to give up. She said to do the best you can and place your trust in God, that He will do the rest."*

I shared Mother Teresa's story with my father. He exclaimed, "That is a beautiful story and it certainly reinforces your concept of miracles." Then he told me a wonderful story in Judaic lore which transmits the same message:

*A certain Rabbi Akiba was traveling by donkey between two towns. As evening fell, he sought lodging at the only inn available. To his dismay, he was turned away because the inn was full. The townspeople did not make any other place available to him, so he was forced to bed down in an adjacent field on the outskirts of the town.*

*During the night, a storm arose. The wind blew out his lantern and knocked down his shelter; lightening struck, killing his donkey. Alas, he surveyed his misfortune and prayed to God. He couldn't understand why such a calamity should befall him.*

*In the morning, he walked the distance back to the town, and to his amazement, found that the town had been pillaged by bandits. They had killed many of the inhabitants. It was then that he thanked God and asked for divine forgiveness for not trusting in the Lord. What he had bemoaned as a misfortune was really a miracle.*

To me, miracles and positive thinking go hand in hand. I believe that miracles can happen when we open our hearts to their possibility. In my life I have repeatedly asked in affirmations and prayers for certain things. I never know when, but I always believe that somehow what I ask for will happen in divine order.

I have always prayed for the safety of family and friends; and I can tell you from personal experience that prayer, positive thinking, visualization and miracles are connected. I'd like to share three brief personal stories – that occurred within the same time period – that I would classify as miracles.

*The first occurred at the summer home of my first husband's parents. I was swinging with my 3-year-old daughter, Laura, in my arms. We were on a wooden swing that was supported by large beams. At one point I looked up and saw the cross beam above us start to give way. I attempted to jump out of the seat as the beam came crashing down. I managed to protect Laura, who only received a swollen lip from the impact. I, however, received a gash on my forehead. We came within inches of being seriously injured. A protective hand maneuvered us out of harm's way that afternoon.*

*A second near-death incident occurred on the highway shortly after the swing mishap. My car veered off the road and headed toward a steep embankment. I turned the steering wheel abruptly, hit the brakes and did a 180 degree turn, coming to rest on the other side of the road. My young daughter, unhurt and undisturbed, was quietly sleeping in the back seat. She was oblivious to what had just happened.*

*The third miracle arose when I was in the car alone. A large truck had just passed me and large sheets of ice hurled off the truck onto my windshield,*

*shattering the glass on the driver's side. As I slid to a*
*stop in the median, I looked down at my hands, arms*
*and chest. Glass and ice covered my upper body, but*
*my hands and face were miraculously untouched.*

In all three of these cases the sequence of events happened so fast that I honestly believe I couldn't have gotten out of the difficulty under my own power. I believe that in each case there was a message for me. My life needed some course corrections and I considered these warnings to take action. My father says I was surrounded by miracles. He believes there is always an invisible order within chaos, that nothing functions haphazardly. "How else does one explain your survival?" he asks. "You were surrounded by angels. You couldn't see them, but they were there."

I've often wondered about angels, their existence and their role in miracles. I think about the TV program "Touched By An Angel" and its message that all of us have guardian angels, and are surrounded by angels. I remembered Terry Barts and wondered if an angel assisted in Terry's transition.

*Terry Barts was the youth pastor at Glad Tidings*
*Pentecostal Holiness Church in our community and*
*was instrumental in helping teens who were in trou-*
*ble. Terry was larger than life and such an*
*inspiration. He was on my program often. He created*
*the Lighthouse, a place where teenagers can meet.*
*Terry explained it, "What we're trying to do is have a*
*positive place, a place where teenagers can be them-*
*selves, where they can be honest, a place where they*
*realize that the adults who are there are there because*
*they love these kids. "They accept these kids and they*
*don't try to straighten them out or try to tell them that*
*'this is what you should do' or, 'this is what you*

*should not do' within the confines of certain rules. We do programs like 180. It's derived from the term and we ask kids to turn 180 degrees in their life. We help them understand that being positive and being forthright and making good choices is a lot of fun. It's a very positive atmosphere and I think it's a lot of fun myself. I receive a lot more than I give."*

*Terry Barts had a heart attack and died while at the Lighthouse playing basketball in the space he created, surrounded by friends and family. It was such a great loss to the community. Shortly after Terry's death, I interviewed Dr. Lester Sauvage, cardiac surgeon, founder of Hope Heart Institute, a leading institution for heart research, and author of You Can Beat Heart Disease and The Open Heart. I mentioned Terry, and how he symbolized "the open heart." I said to him, "He just keeled over and died!" Dr. Sauvage's response was, "And went straight to heaven and that's not bad!"*

Dr. Sauvage's passion, mission and motto are all wrapped into one. He said, "We can change this world in one generation if we have the courage and will to do so. We can do that by putting God's love to full action in our lives." This is what Terry preached. I can just hear Terry saying, "Amen, brother!"

When I told my father about Terry Barts and how he died, my father spontaneously said, "That's the miracle. Miracles are not necessarily fairy tales. The miracle is that God took him. God needed him somewhere. Who knows what type of person might be a *lamed-vovnick.*"

Miracles come in many forms. Oftentimes they appear in ways that aren't immediately apparent. No one knows why God took Terry. The way Terry died was so unexpected. I'd like to think the way my father thought of it – God needed Terry somewhere. God needed a *lamed-vovnick* somewhere else.

## *Is It Coincidence, Chance or Miracle?*

*Every memorable act in the history of the world is a triumph of enthusiasm. Nothing great was ever achieved without it because it gives any challenge or any occupation, no matter how frightening or difficult, a new meaning. Without enthusiasm you are doomed to a life of mediocrity, but with it you can accomplish miracles.*

(Og Mandino)

*T*here are instances in our lives when we cannot understand why certain things happen. Some people call them coincidences. Others believe they are miracles. Still others discount them as mere chance. Let me share a personal experience with you. You decide whether it's a coincidence, chance or miracle.

*I was living in the Boston area, and my daughter Laura, was about three years old. Our steady babysitter was a family friend. One day I let her borrow my car to run an errand. She came from a large family, and when she stopped at her house, one of her older brothers "took" the car.*

*I spent the whole next day on the phone with the police, frantically trying to locate my car. In despera-*

211

*tion, I called my father, who was working in New York City. He reassured me that no matter how things turned out, everything was going to be okay. The day after we spoke, in the late afternoon, my father called me and said, 'You are not going to believe what I'm about to tell you. Today, instead of walking my usual route to the parking lot, I walked down a different street and there was your car on this side street in the middle of downtown Manhattan!" This was a 'one in a million shot,' to use my father's words at the time, and I was stunned but also thrilled that my father found my car.*

*He immediately called the police. When the officers got there, they decided to remove the distributor so no one could start the car. My father took the distributor with him and called me as soon as he got home. Since my father worked in New York City, he said he would go back the next morning to make arrangements to get my car back home.*

*The next morning, when my father went to the street where the car had been parked, the car was gone. When he called to tell me the bad news, I told him the good news! My babysitter's older brother, after taking my car on a joyride, realized his mistake and returned it to me in Boston. She told me later how panicked he was when he realized the distributor was missing. We eventually got it all worked out, but what makes this story so amazing is that my father was able to find my car 250 miles from home in a city of tens of millions of people. The chances of coincidentally finding his daughter's stolen car were miraculous.*

I believe there was a higher power at work. I believe it was fueled by prayer, trust and interconnectedness. I believe it included the power of a father's love for his daughter. My father and I have always had a deep connection, a psychic connection of sorts. It was ironic that he would be the one to find my car, especially under the peculiar circumstances. I'm still amazed when I think about the extraordinary ramifications of my "lost car" miracle.

What if coincidences and chance are the tools miracles use to present themselves? If they are, I've got the perfect coincidental miracle to share with you. I call it the Miracle Story. It's one of those 'one-in-a-million shots.' Here's what happened:

*I was in the final stages of producing a television documentary on Positive Aging in Winston-Salem, North Carolina. We were going to end the documentary with an older gentleman who was featured in the closing segment. He had brought photographs he thought would be perfect for the ending. When we disagreed about several of his selections, he became difficult. He finally stormed out of the studio, leaving me without a completed documentary and without very much time to find available talent.*

*I sat in the conference room wondering how on earth I was going to fix the broken ending, when the receptionist entered the conference room unannounced. She was carrying a package addressed to me. I was flabbergasted. I only worked in the studio once a month. Any mail addressed to me usually laid in my in-box, awaiting my arrival. This particular package arrived and was delivered to me the day I was there.*

*The package contained a national press release from Houston, Texas announcing a senior sports classics competition. One of the people featured was the 102-year-old golfer named Harley Potter who you*

213

*met in Chapter Five. He was from – you guessed it – Winston Salem. I'm sitting in a conference room at the Fox TV affiliate in Winston-Salem approximately twenty minutes away from an octogenarian who would be the perfect closing story for my documentary.*

*I called his 75 year-old daughter and she arranged for me to meet them at the local club where he played golf almost daily. The rest, as they say, is history – or should I say miraculous history. When events like this unfold, I believe there has to be a guiding hand that waves some sort of cosmic wand, which transforms ordinary experiences into extraordinary events.*

My husband, Antonio, calls these miraculous transformations "spiritual economics." He says, "Spiritual economics is God's way of producing win-win solutions without letting time, distance and geography interfere with important human connections."

The following personal story illustrates this divine connection.

*During one of my parents' visits, we got a phone call from the American Society of Plastic Surgeons (ASPS) announcing that Antonio and I had won the Media Excellence Award for his radio program, "Plastic Surgery Today," which I produce. The wonderful thing about the announcement was its timing. My parents were with us when we got the news. They got to share the moment.*

*My parents are in their eighties and can only visit us a couple of times a year. To have had them in the same room with us when we got the call was thrilling, to say the least. I have always dreamed of receiving recognition for my achievements with my parents present. The Media Excellence Award was a dream come true for two very special reasons which are outlined below.*

*We were the recipients of a double miracle. When we received the actual award at the annual scientific meeting of the ASPS, the location for the year 2001 "happened to be" in Orlando, Florida, which was within driving distance for my parents. So they and Antonio's mother, who also lives in Florida, were able to be present at our awards ceremony.*

*Another part of that miracle was that, during the opening ceremonies of the annual meeting, the president of the ASPS at that time unexpectedly recognized Antonio as an unsung hero for his radio program.*

I believe the "spiritual economics" of miracles were at work here, making it possible for all of us to be in the same place at the same time for the same event. I have shared this double miracle story with you because I believe we receive multiple miracles every day in the form of coincidences and chances.

# *Let Miracles Point the Way*

We must not allow the clock and the
calendar to blind us to the fact that each
moment of life is a miracle. (H. G. Wells.)

*M*iracles point the way to more miracles, to more
coincidences, to more happenstances, to more
synchronous experiences and to more harmonious events.
"The world is full of wonders and miracles," says Israel
Baal Shem, "but mankind takes its little hand and covers its
eyes and sees nothing." Miracles are all around us, all we
have to do is allow the miraculous to point the way.

The following story is about Karen Yuskaitis' amazing
encounter with a raging Colorado wild fire.

*The fire had been started accidentally by a care-
less camper and turned into an inferno that consumed
an area five miles wide and twenty-two miles long.
Although much of the forest land was devastated, her
property, the cabin tepee and sweat lodge were spared
and left intact.*

*Forty Indian firefighters had been sent as part of
the National Firefighter Team to dig trenches and
construct fire lanes and to create a fire break around
her property. Fortunately, their heroic efforts to contain the fire saved her property.*

*When Karen was first allowed to return to her
property, she found a severely burned and blinded
rabbit that had taken refuge in the protection and
shade under her house. Feeling that there already had
been so much devastation, she wanted to do anything
she could to save something living, even something as*

216

*seemingly insignificant as a rodent rabbit. When I asked Karen why the rabbit was so important to her, she replied, "The rabbit had such a strong will to live. It later turned out that she was carrying babies, in fact nine babies in all. Sadly, the trauma of the fire resulted in them all being stillborn. It was the relationship with the rabbit that took me out of my personal saga of loss and devastation surrounding me all over the mountain."*

*Recognizing and acknowledging the many miracles that she was blessed with, Karen questioned why she was the recipient of such good fortune. She shared, "A Native American Indian told me that I should say prayers and give an offering. Then he said to me, 'Maybe you already did.' When I questioned what he meant, he said that I had given a great gift already when earlier that summer I had purchased a playground for the children of Pine Ridge Reservation I was told later that the playground had been a lifelong dream of Jimmy Dubray, the spiritual leader of the Ogalala Sioux."*

I believe that Karen's work for the people of the reservation was rewarded by Jimmy Dubray, even after he died, and may have had something to do with her property being saved.

Ralph Waldo Emerson said, "Miracles refuse to be analyzed." Robert Schuller believes, "Impossible situations can become possible miracles." Peggy Noonan insists that, "Miracles exist in part as gifts and in part as clues that there is something beyond the flat world we see." George Bernard Shaw described them as, "Phenomena we can't explain." Henry Christopher Bailey maintains that "In order to be a realist you must believe in miracles."

The next miracle story is Tiffany Klein's story as she tells it:

*It was a rainy Saturday night in mid-November 1986. I had only had my 1972 Beetle for 8 months, as well as my license. Like any other 16 year old, I was out to have a fun night. I went to a party at a friend's house. I stayed there for about 3 hours, but something told me not to drink that night. A girlfriend asked me for a ride home, but I told her that I was already late and did not have time to take her home.*

*It was pouring buckets of rain by the time I left. Seat belts were not a required thing in 1986, but I wore mine because of the fear that my dad would catch me without it and take my car way. The seat belt on the driver's side did not fit properly; it was very loose. The seat belt on the passenger side did not work at all.*

*I turned onto the main road, which was only one lane each way. Not even 10 seconds later, I hit a puddle and, being an inexperienced driver, panicked and hit the brakes. As I began to slip and slide around on the road, I counteracted and overcorrected and began to flip down the road. I recall flipping at least 8 times.*

*The next thing I remember was being right side up in between two trees. One tree was so close to the passenger side that you could not even open the door. I got out of the car and remember feeling lost. The paramedics were there as well as the fire department. The police officer was asking me all kinds of questions about my family and phone numbers, checking to see if I had been drinking or was in shock. The car was completely totaled. The top was smashed in, the front was at the windshield, the back glass had popped out and was lying in one piece on the ground.*

*When my mom saw me, she said that there must have been angels in the car with pillows. The paramedic was stunned that I even made it out alive, much less able to get in the car to go home with my mom.*

*This really brought my mom and I much closer. It also gave me an appreciation for life that I never knew before. Never take anything for granted; never leave someone you love without saying "I love you," because you might not see them again; and live life to its fullest, because you only get one turn in this crazy world.*

Before we leave the subject of miracles, I've got to share one more amazing miracle story. It was told to me by Bil Holton, President of Liberty Publishing Group, the publisher of this book. It is the perfect example of Rev. Schuller's belief that "impossible situations can turn into possible miracles."

*When Bil was a youngster, he lived in a rural neighborhood that was situated adjacent to an open air incinerator. The children were fascinated by the large trucks and machinery associated with the operation of this outdoor furnace, and although they had been forbidden to play around it, they saw it as the perfect site for their war games.*

*The incinerator was surrounded on three sides by a three-foot high cement wall. The front section was open to allow trucks access to dump trash into it. The children would square off at each other by kneeling behind the walls so they could shoot at each other with their toy rifles. The smoke from the burning debris made a perfect smoke screen for each army to hide behind.*

*One particular morning, the children were gathered around the incinerator's edge. Suddenly, the groundskeeper came running towards them, shouting at them to leave.*

*The children were used to his censorship and enjoyed the challenge of evading him and then outrunning him whenever he appeared. Bil was one of the oldest youngsters at age twelve, so he and a couple of older boys would stay as long as they could, taunting him before they sprinted to safety.*

*As he skillfully dodged the outstretched arm of the groundskeeper, Bil left himself little room to negotiate his angle around one section of the incinerator wall. He tripped over the edge of the wall and to the horror of everyone present, fell into the incinerator. A few moments later, those nearest stood in stunned silence as they saw Bil's hands grab the top of the three foot high cement lip on the other side of the incinerator–a distance of some twenty feet from where he had fallen backwards into the blazing inferno.*

*He had lost the toy rifle he was carrying, along with his ball cap. Both were reduced to ashes. He explained to me that when he fell into the incinerator, he felt something lift him and carry him across to the other side. He felt like he was being transported by an unseen force from one end of the fiery furnace to the other.*

*The kids, who are all adults now, still talk about Bil's incredible levitational feat. Bil revisited the site of his "miracle" when he was in his late teens. He described the open space of the incinerator as twenty-five feet by twenty-five. "No way could I have leaped across it on my own," he explains. "From a running start as an adult, I couldn't jump that far. How a twelve-year old, falling backwards into an open pit could have survived such a fall is still beyond belief.*

220

*It was a miracle. I don't know any other suitable explanation."*

*I asked him what affect such an experience has had on his life. He responded without any hesitation, "Miracles like the one I experienced cause people to ask, 'Why me? Why was I saved? Did God save me for a special purpose?' My answer has been the same for over forty years – God truly works in mysterious ways. Although we may not be able to understand the substance and timing of a divine intervention, I believe we grow into a greater understanding of our relationship with the divine. I have come to believe that divine beings intervene in human affairs much more often than we think. The miracle at the incinerator gave me a second chance. I am absolutely convinced that a twelve-year-old boy felt the presence of an invisible force that lifted him out of danger. Ever since that supernatural event, I have believed in miracle power."*

All of the miracle stories in this book seem to have one thing in common: Everyone experienced an extraordinary event that couldn't be fully explained by the known rules of science, logic and chance. Each person experienced an awesome truth – what seemed impossible became possible. The incomprehensible became real and the miraculous became a verifiable event.

You may not have experienced a miracle of the magnitude in these stories, and you may feel that chance and logic are the mind's way of discounting the miraculous. But we've all experienced those "coincidences" when someone we have just been thinking about calls us, we bump into the person we really needed to talk to, we find the right thing at exactly the right time, or we avoid a mishap by seconds. I believe that those are miracles, and that we can create them by our thoughts. If you really want something, ask for it, pray for it, truly believe you will receive it, and then wait for something to happen. You don't have to actively work at it, because something greater than you is at work here. I feel that something is God.

Give thanks for those little miracles when they happen because they open the door to the big miracles. When you let miracles point the way, you know you're on the right path. Pathfinding is miracle producing. The two go hand in hand.

## *Positive Pollination*

*List:*
- ❖ Coincidences in your life that to you are more than chance or luck.
- ❖ Miraculous events in your own life that have no logical explanation.
- ❖ A "miracle worker" or miracle situation you know or have read about.

*Reflect on:*
- ❖ What makes a miracle a miracle.
- ❖ Whether coincidences and chance should be called miracles.
- ❖ The times miracles have pointed the way for major changes in your life.

# Conclusion

*T*hrough conversations and reflections with my father, I have gained an understanding of my parents' choices and of the core beliefs and values that defined our family. Through the stimulating conversations I've had with the guests I've interviewed on my shows over the past twenty years, I've gained extraordinary insights from extraordinary people. And from both I have woven my own tapestry of positive living principles.

It is my sincere hope that through these principles, you will be able to acknowledge your own heritage and find ancestral mirrors for your own traits, talents and abilities. As you embrace each new day, I hope you will use each precious moment as a platform for self-development and human service. When you use your imperfections to perfect your life, you'll be able to learn from your mistakes and rewrite your personal narrative so you can blaze your own path toward positive living.

I hope you'll use your innate gifts, talents and abilities to encourage others to use their own special qualities to make this world a better place for all of us. I truly believe that if you focus on the positive and surround yourself with positive people, you will find the balance, peace and harmony you seek.

As you work at protecting and respecting priceless relationships, you will recognize how essential they are to your continued growth and well-being. And when you find the miraculous in the ordinary, you will feel an indescribable divine presence as it graces your everyday life and experiences.

I hope you will re-read my father's story about the caretaker in the foreword to this book – because it is your story. It is the reason I wrote this book.

"Ah," says the caretaker, "If I could write, I'd still be a caretaker."

If I take the liberty of paraphrasing the wise caretaker in accordance with the theme for this book, he might just as well have said:

"Ah! If you could have been someone else, you'd still be someone else, and not yourself."

But you are you. You must find your own path. It's there waiting for you. I believe these seven principles for positive living can help accelerate your path to peace, happiness, prosperity and selfhood. "Everybody's trip is different," my father reminds us. "because we are all on the road called life." And that road, the road toward selfhood, can only be gained through positive living.

# Bibliography

Bach, Richard. Illusions: Adventures of a Reluctant Messiah. New York: Dell Publishing Co., Inc., 1977.

Beattie, Melody. Journey to the Heart. New York: HarperSanFranciso, 1996.

Berndt, Jodie. Celebration of Miracles: An Intriguing Look at the Miraculous Events that Touch Our Lives. Nashville: Thomas Nelson Inc. Publishers, 1995.

Bloomfield, Harold, M.D. with Phillip Goldberg. Making Peace with Your Past: The Six Essential Steps to Enjoying a Great Future. New York: Harper Collins Publishers, 2000. www.haroldbloomfield.com

Bloomfield, Harold H. and Robert Kory. Holistic Way to Health and Happiness. New York: Simon and Schuster, 1978.

Bolles, Richard N. How to Find Your Mission in Life. Berkeley, California: Ten Speed Press, 2000.

---. Job-Hunting on the Internet. Berkeley, California: Ten Speed Press, 2001. www.jobhuntersbible.com

---. What Color is Your Parachute? Berkeley, California: Ten Speed Press, 2002.

Bolt, Stephen R. Money for Life. Nashville: VFN Publishing, 2000. www.moneyandvalues.com

Borysenko, Joan,. Guilt Is The Teacher, Love Is The Lesson. New York: Warner Books, Inc., 1990. www.joanborysenko.com

Bramson, Robert M., Coping With Difficult People. New York: Dell Publishing, 1981.

Breathnach, Sarah Ban. Simple Abundance: A Daybook of Comfort and Joy. New York: Warner Books, 1995. www.simpleabundance.com

---. Something More: Excavating Your Authentic Self. New York: Warner Books, 1998.

Bry, Adelaide. Learning to Love Forever. New York: MacMillan Publishing Company, 1982.

225

---. Visualization: Directing the Movies of Your Mind. Videotape. New York: MacMillan Publishing Company, 1984.

Buscaglia, Leo F.,. Living, Loving and Learning. Connecticut: Fawcett Books, 1990.

Cameron, Julia. The Artist's Way: A Spiritual Path to Higher Creativity. New York: G.P. Putnam's Sons, 1992.

Carson, Lillian,. The Essential Grandparent: A Guide To Making A Difference. Deerfield Beach, Florida: Health Communications, 1996.
www.essentialgrandparent.com

Carlson, Richard. Don't Sweat the Small Stuff...and It's All Small Stuff. New York: Hyperion, 1997
www.dontsweat.com.

Collins, Terah Katherine. Western Guide to Feng Shui: Creating Balance, Harmony, Prosperity in Your Environment. Carlsbed, California: Hay House, 1999.

Covey, Stephen R. The 7 Habits of Highly Effective People: Powerful Lessons in Personal Change. New York: Simon and Schuster, 1989
www.franklincovey.com.

---. Principle-Centered Leadership. New York: Simon and Schuster, 1991.

Curley, Thomas. Masters Among Us. Victoria: Trafford Publishing, 2000.

Dahl, Lynda with Cathleen Daelyn. The Book of Fallacies: A Little Primer of New Thought. Portsmouth, Maine: Moment Point Press, 2001.
www.momentpoint.com

Dossey, Donald E., Holiday Folklore, Phobias and Fun: Mythical Origins, Scientific Treatments and Superstitious "Cures". Los Angeles: Outcomes Unlimited Press, Inc., 1992.

---. Keying: The Power of Positive Feelings. Los Angeles: Outcomes Unlimited Press, Inc., 1989.

Dytchwald, Ken. Age Wave: How the Most Important Trend of Our Time Will Change Your Future. New York: Bantam Books, 1990.

Eadie, Betty J. The Ripple Effect Our Harvest. Seattle: Onjinjinkta Publishing, 1999.
www.embracedbythelight.com

# Bibliography

Falcon, Rabbi Ted, A Journey of Awakening: 49 Steps from Enslavement to Freedom. Seattle: Skynear Press, n.d. www.betalef.org

---. Journey of Awareness: Using the Kabbalistic Tree of Life in Jewish Meditation. Seattle: Skynear Press, 1999.

Farson, Richard and Ralph Keys. Whoever Makes the Most Mistakes WINS. New York: FREE Press, 2002.

Feldman, Ron H. Fundamentals of Jewish Mysticism and Kabbalah. Freedom,California: Crossing Press, 1999.

Foyder, Joan Ellen. Family Caregivers Guide.Cincinnati: Kendall-Futuro, 1986.

Frankl, Viktor E. Man's Search for Meaning. New York: Simon and Schuster, 1977.

Garrett, J.T. Meditations with The Cherokee. Vermont: Bear & Company, 2001.

Garrett, J.T. and Michael Garrett. Medicine of the Cherokee. Santa Fe: Bear and Company Publishing, 1996.

Gawain, Shakti. Living in the Light. Mill Valley, California: Whatever Publishing, Inc., 1986. www.shaktigawain.com

Gelb, Michael J. Discover Your Genius. New York: HarperCollins Publishers, 2002 www.michaelgelb.com

---. How to Think Like Leonardo daVinci.. New York: Dell Publishing, 1998.

Gelissen, Rena Kornreich with Heather Dune Macadam.. Rena's Promise. Boston: Beacon Press, 1995. www.historyplace.com/bookshop/promise.htm

George, Henry. Progress & Poverty. New York: Robert Schalkenbach Foundation, 1996.

Gibran, Kahlil. The Prophet.. New York: Alfred A. Knopf. 1965.

Goodman, Joel. Laffirmations. Deerfield Beach, Florida: Health Communications Inc., 1995. www.humorproject.com

Gros, Tatjana and Primoz S'koberne. Crosses of Light and Other Miracles. CDK Institute, Ljubljana, 1999.

Harder, David. The Truth About Work: Making a Life, Not a Living. Deerfield Beach, Florida: Health Communications Inc., 1997.

Hay, Louise L. You Can Heal Your Life. Carlsbed, California: Hay House, 1984.
www.hayhouse.org

Hertz Pentateuch. London: Soncinel Press, 1992.

Hill, Napoleon and Clement W Stone. Success Through a Positive Mental Attitude. Englewood Cliffs, New Jersey: Prentice-Hall, Inc., 1960.
www.naphill.org

Holton, Bil and Cher Holton. The Manager's Short Course to a Long Career. Raleigh, North Carolina: 1999.
www.holtonconsulting.com

Holton, Cher. Living At The Speed of Life: Staying in Control in a World Gone Bonkers! Raleigh, North Carolina: Liberty Publishing Group, 1999.

HOPE Magazine. Jon Wilson, Publisher, Brookline, Maine
www.hopemag.com.

Hutchinson, Marcia Germaine. 200 Ways To Love The Body You Have. Freedom, California: The Crossing Press, 1999.

Irwin, Bill. Blind Courage. Waco, Texas: WRS Publishing, 1993.
www.billirwin.com

Johnson, Spencer. The Precious Present. New York: Doubleday, 1992.

---. Who Moved My Cheese? New York: G.P. Putnam's Sons, 1998.
www.whomovedmycheese.com

Kabat-Zinn, Jon. Wherever You Go, There You Are. New York: Hyperion Books, 1994.
www.mindfulnesstapes.com

Kassey, Karen Grace. Health Intuition: A Simple Guide to Greater Well-Being. Center City, Minnesota: Hazelden Information & Educational Services, 2000.
www.healthintuition.com

Kersey, Cynthia. Unstoppable. Naperville, Illinois: Sourcebook, Inc., 1998. www.unstoppable.net

Kingsbury, Karen. A Treasury of Miracles for Women: True Stories of God's Presence Today. New York: Warner Books, 2002.

# Bibliography

Knaus, William J. Take Charge Now! Powerful Techniques for
Breaking The Blame Habit. New York: John Wiley & Sons, Inc., 2000.

Kreidman, Ellen. Light His Fire: How to Keep Your Man Passionately
and Hopelessly in Love with You. New York: Dell Publishing
Company, 1991
www.lightyourfire.com.

---. Light Her Fire: How to Ignite Passion, Joy, and Excitement in the
Woman you Love. New York: Dell Publishing Company, 1992.

Kushner, Harold S. When Bad Things Happen to Good People. New
York: Avon, 1997.

---. Living a Life That Matters. New York: Avon, 2001.

Kyle, David T. The Four Powers of Leadership. Deerfield Beach,
Florida: Health Communications, Inc., 1998.
www.lindandkyle.com

Leech, Thomas. Say It Like Shakespeare. New York: Mc-Graw-Hill, 2001.
www.sayitlikeshakespeare.com

Levey, Joel and Michelle Levey. Living in Balance: A Dynamic
Approach for Creating Harmony and Balance in a Chaotic World.
Berkeley: Conari Press, Jan. 1998.
www.wisdomatwork.com

Levinson, Steve, and Pete C. Greider. Following Through: A
Revolutionary New Model for Finishing Whatever you Start. New
York: Kensington Books, 1998.

Lewis, Michael. Altering Fate: Why the Past Does Not Predict the
Future. New York: The Guilford Press, 1997.

Lima, David R. The Love Workbook: A Guide To Happiness In Your
Personal Relationships. Mentor, Ohio: Super Six Publishers, 1988,
1999. www.sillymind.com

---. The Silly Mind: Learning to Take Life More or Less Seriously.
Mentor, Ohio: Super Six Publishers, 2001.

Maher, Barry. Filling the Glass: The Skeptic's Guide to Positive
Thinking in Business. Chicago: Dearborn Trade, 2001.
www.barrymaher.com

McBride, Tracey. Frugal Luxuries: Simple Pleasure to Enhance Your
Life and Comfort Your Soul. New York: Bantam Books, 1997.
www.frugalluxuries.com

McCormick, Adele von Rust and Marlena DeborahMcCormick..
Horse Sense and the Human Heart: What Horses Can Teach Us
About Trust, Bonding, Creativity and Spirituality. Deerfield Beach,
Florida: Health Communications, Inc., 1997.

Millman, Dan. No Ordinary Moments. Tibiron, California: HJ
Kramer, Inc., 1992.
www.danmillman.com

---. Pathways to the Soul. Videotape. n.p., n.d.

Misner, Ivan R and Don, Morgan. Masters of Networking: Building
Relationships for Your Pocketbook and Soul. Marietta, Georgia: Bard
Press, 2000.
www.bni.com

Moore, Thomas. Care of the Soul: A Guide for Cultivating Depth and
Sacredness In Everyday Life. New York: HarperCollins Publishers,
Inc., 1992.
www.wellmedia.com/collection/spirit/moore2.html.

---. Soul Mates: Honoring the Mysteries of Love and Relationships.
New York: Harper Perennial, 1994.

---. The Re-Enchantment of Everyday Life. New York: HarperCollins
Publishers, Inc., 1997

Moyer, Bill. Healing and The Mind. New York: Bantam, Doubleday,
Dell Publishing Group, Inc., 1993.

Myss Caroline. Anatomy of the Spirit: The Seven Stages of Power
and Healing. New York: Random House, 1997.
www.myss.com

---. Energy Anatomy: The Science of Personal Power, Spirituality and
Health. Boulder, Colorado: Sounds True Audiotapes, 1996.

Naisbitt, John. Megatrends. New York: Warner Books, 1982, 1984.
www.naisbitt.com

Nukols, Cardwell C. and Bill Chickering. Healing An Angry Heart.
Deerfield Beach, Florida: Health Communications, Inc., 1998.

NurrieStearns, Rick, Mary NurrieStearns, and Melissa West. Soulful
Living: The Process of Personal Transformation. Deerfield Beach,
Florida: Health Communications, Inc., 1999.
www.personaltransformation.com

# *Bibliography*

Ornish, Dean. Dr. Dean Ornish's Program for Reversing Heart Disease: The Only System Scientifically Proven to Reverse Heart Disease Without Drugs or Surgery. New York: Ballentine Books, 1996.
www.ornish.com

---. Love & Survival: 8 Pathways to Intimacy and Health. New York: Harper Collins, 1999.

---. Eat More, Weigh Less: Dr. Dean Ornish's Life Choice Program for Losing Weight Safely While Eating Abundantly. New York: Quill, 2000.

Patent, Arnold M. You Can Have It All. New York: Money Mastery Publishing, 1984.

Parrott, Les and Leslie Parrott. When Bad Things Happen To Good Marriages. Great Rapids, Michigan: Zondervan Publishing House, 2001. www.RealRelationships.com

Paul, Jordan, Ph.D. and Margaret Paul. Do I Have To Give Up Me To Be Loved By You? Center City, Minnesota: Hazelden, 1983.
www.innerbondng.com

---. Do I Have To Give Up Me To Be Loved by God? Deerfield Beach, Florida: Health Communications, Inc.,1999.

Pavuk, Stephen and Pamela Pavuk. The Story of a Lifetime. Sante Fe, New Mexico: Triangle Publishers, 2000.
www.thestoryofalifetime.com

Peck, M. Scott. The Road Less Traveled: A New Psychology of Love, Traditional Values and Spiritual Growth. New York: Simon & Schuster, 1978.
www.scottpeck.com

---. Further Along the Road Less Traveled: The Unending Journey Toward Spiritual Growth. New York: Simon & Schuster, 1993.

---. The Road Less Traveled and Beyond: Spiritual Growth in an Age of Anxiety. New York: Simon & Schuster, 1997.

Peterson, Wayne S. Extraordinary Times, Extraordinary Beings: Experiences of an American Diplomat with Maitreya and the Masters of Wisdom. Henderson, NV: Emergence Press, 2001.

Pierce, Linda Breen. Choosing Simplicity: Real People Finding Peace and Fulfillment in a Complex World. Carmel, California: Gallagher Press, 2000.
www.gallagherpress.com

Ponder, Catherine. Open Your Mind to Prosperity. Marina Del Ray: DeVorss and Company, 1983.

Positive Press. <http://www.positivepress.com>

Prentiss, Chris. The Little Book of Secrets. California: Power Press, 2000.

Price, John Randolph. The Super Beings. Boerne, Texas: Quartus Books, 1981.
www.quartus.org

Raskin, Patricia. Success, Your Dream and You: A Guide To Personal Marketing. Malibu, California: Roundtable Publishing, Inc., 1991.

---. Creative Marketing: A Workbook on Marketing for the Massage Therapist. Cheshire, Connecticut: Raskin Resources, 1993.
www.raskinresources.com

Redfield, James. The Tenth Insight: Holding the Vision. New York: Warner Books, Inc., 1996.
www.celestinevision.com

---. The Celestine Prophecy: An Adventure. New York: Warner Books Inc., 1997.

---. The Celestine Vision: Living the New Spiritual Awareness. New York: Warner Books Inc., 1997.

Remen, Rachel Naomi. My Grandfather's Blessings: Stories of Strength, Refuge, and Belonging. New York: Riverhead Books, 2000.

Riley, Linda. The Call To Love. Wheaton, Illinois: Tyndale House Publishers, Inc. 2000.
www.learntolove.org

Robbins, Anthony. Unlimited Power. New York: Fawcett Columbine, 1986.
www.tonyrobbins.com

Roman, Sanaya and Duane Packer. Creating Money: Keys to Abundance. Tiberon, California: HJ Kramer Inc., 1988.

Rosenfield, Isadore. Live Now, Age Later: Proven Ways to Slow Down the Clock. New York: Warner Books, Inc., 1999.

Ross, Ruth. Prospering Woman. Mill Valley, California: Whatever Publishing, Inc., 1982.

Ryan, Regina Sara and John W. Travis. Wellness Workbook. Second Edition. Berkeley, California: Ten Speed Press, 1988.

# *Bibliography*

Samuels, Michael, and Mary Rockwood Lane. Spirit Body Healing.
Ontario, Canada: John Wiley and Sons, Inc., 2000.
www.spiritbodyhealing.com

Sauvage, Lester R. Better Life Diet: How to Live a Long and Youthful
Life. Seattle: Better Life Press, 2001
www.drsauvage.com

Sauvage, Lester, R. and His Patients. The Open Heart: Secret To
Happiness. Seattle: Better Life Press, 1998.

Schultz, Mona Lisa. Awakening Intuition. New York: Crown
Publishers, Inc., 1998.

Schwarzbein, Diana and Nancy Deville. The Schwarzbein Principle:
The Truth About Losing Weight, Being Healthy and Feeling
Younger. Deerfield Beach, Florida: Health Communications, Inc.,
1999.
www.drhormone.com

Seaward, Brian Luke. The Art Of Calm: Relaxation Through the Five
Senses. Deerfield Beach, Florida: Health Communications, Inc.,
1999.
www.brianlukeseaward.net

Sherven, Judith and James Sniechowski. Be Loved For Who You
Really Are. Los Angeles: Renaissance Books, 2001.
www.themagicofdifferences.com

---. Opening to Love 365 Days a Year. Deerfield Beach, Florida:
Health Communications, Inc., 2000.

---. The New Intimacy.Deerfield Beach, Florida: Health
Communications, Inc., 1997.

Sivertsen, Linda. Lives Charmed: Intimate Conversations with
Extraordinary People. Deerfield Beach, Florida: Health
Communications Inc., 1998.

Solart, Ellen Fritz. Living Inside Out: Saying Yes to the Inner Voice.
Mayer, Arizona: Desert Sage Publishing, 1999.

Stone, Clement W. The Success System That Never Fails. Englewood
Cliffs, New Jersey: Prentice-Hall, Inc., 1962.

Straub, Gail. Circle of Compassion. Boston: Journey Editions, 2001.
www.empowermenttraining.com

---. The Rhythm of Compassion: Caring For Self Connecting With
Society. Boston: Tuttle Publishing, 2000.

Straub, Gail and David Gershon. Empowerment: The Art of Creating Your Life As You Want It. New York: Dell Publishing, 1989.

Sullivan, Steve D. Selling At Mach 1. Ridgefield, Connecticut: Motivational Resources, 1994.

Tartaglia, Louis A. The Great Wing: A Parable. Hillsboro, Oregon: Beyond Words Publishing, Inc., 1997.
www.tartaglia.com

---. Flawless: The Ten Most Common Character Flaws and What You Can Do About Them. New York: Eagle Brook, William and Morrow and Company, Inc., 1999.

Tartaglia, Louis A. and Father Angelo Scolozzi, with Mother Teresa.. Thirsting for God: The Spiritual Lessons of Mother Teresa. Audiotape. Niles, Illinois: Nightingale-Conant Corp., 2001.

Twerski, Abraham J. Life's Too Short: Pull the Plug on Self-Defeating Behavior and Turn on the Power of Self-Esteem. New York: St. Martin's Press,1995.
www.12steps2selfesteem.com

---. Addictive Thinking. Center City, Minnesota: Hazelden, 1990, 1997.

---. The Enemy Within: Confronting Your Challenges in the 21st Century. Brooklyn, New York: Shaar Press Publications, 2002.

Van Ekeren, Glenn. 12 Simple Secrets Of Happiness: Finding Joy In Everyday Relationships. Paramus, New Jersey: Prentice Hall Press, 2000.

Waldman, Jackie with Janis Leibs Dworki . The Courage to Give. Berkeley, California: Conari Press, 1999.

Waldman, Jackie with Brenda Welchlin and Karen Frost. America, September 11th The Courage to Give. Berkeley, California: Conari Press, 2001.

Waldman, Jackie. Teens with the Courage to Give. Berkeley, California: Conari Press, 2000.
www.couragetogive.com

Walsch, Neale Donald. Conversations with God: An Uncommon Dialogue. NY: Putnam Pub Group, 1996.
www.conversationswithgod.org

# Bibliography

Weil, Andrew. Taking Care of Yourself: Strategies for Eating Well, Staying Fit, and Living in Balance. New York: Sounds True, Inc., 2002.
www.drweil.com

---. Eating Well for Optimum Health: The Essential Guide to Bringing Health and Pleasure Back to Eating. New York: HarperTrade, 2001.

---. Natural Health, Natural Medicine. New York: Houghton Mifflin Company, 1998.

Whittaker, Tom. Higher Purpose. Washington, D.C.: LifeLine Press, 2001.
www.tomwhittaker.com

Williams, Mark E. The American Geriatrics Society's Complete Guide To Aging & Health. New York: Harmony Books, 1995.

Woodard, K.L. The Book of Miracles: The Meaning of the Miracle Stories in Christianity, Judaism, Buddhism, Hinduism, and Islam.. NY: Simon & Schuster, 2000.

Yager, Jan. Friendshifts: The Power of Friendship and How It Shapes Our Lives. Stamford, Connecticut: Hannacroix Creek Books, Inc., 1999.
www.janyager.com

---. When Friendship Hurts. New York, Fireside Books, 2002.
www.whenfriendshiphurts.com

Zukav, Gary. The Seat of the Soul.. New York: Simon & Schuster,1990.
www.zukav.com

# About the Author ~

*P*atricia Raskin, president and founder of Raskin Resources, is a media producer/host, speaker and author who serves as a catalyst for creating positive change. For twenty years, she has been hosting and producing media programs that focus on the positive side of life. Patricia originally developed her skills as a teacher and guidance counselor, focusing on prevention, self awareness and positive life skills. As a pioneer in the earliest days of cable television, Patricia created "Positive People" talk shows. Since then she has gone on to produce and host television talk shows and documentaries that have aired on Fox and PBS affiliates.

Patricia interviews nationally acclaimed experts and authors in the areas of self-help, personal growth and inspiration on her call-in radio program, "Positive Living," which is the basis for her newspaper column. Patricia also hosts a weekly radio show, which can be heard on the internet worldwide.

Patricia holds a Masters's degree in Counseling and is the author of *Success, Your Dream and You: A Guide to Personal Marketing* and *Creative Marketing: A Workbook on Marketing for the Massage Therapist*. She received the 2001 Circle of Excellence Media Award from the American Society of Plastic Surgeons for producing the radio program "Plastic Surgery Today," hosted by her husband, plastic surgeon Dr. Antonio Carbonell.

Patricia has been recognized as a "Distinguished Woman of the Year" by the Council for Women in her community.

# Contact Information

Patricia Raskin inspires audiences nationally with her motivational talks and seminars.

Tapes and CDs of guest interviews from Positive Living are available for purchase.

For information about booking Patricia to speak for your organization or association, and for information about her books, as well as the tapes and CDs from her radio show, write or call:

## *Raskin Resources*

P.O. Box 1468
Morehead City, N.C. 28557
800-528-5890 or 252-247-1133

www.raskinresources.com